Embracing the Journey of AI Leadership.

Welcome to The AI Compass: Security, Ethics, and Leadership, a comprehensive guide designed to empower you with the knowledge and insights needed to navigate the complex and evolving world of artificial intelligence. As AI continues to redefine how we live, work, and interact, it becomes increasingly important to lead with both confidence and caution. This book serves not only as a roadmap to understanding AI's foundational concepts and applications but as a call to action to approach AI with the responsibility and vision it demands.

Throughout my career as an AI advocate, entrepreneur, and leader at Kazma Technology and as the founder of ChatWeft, I have witnessed the tremendous capabilities of AI, as well as the ethical dilemmas and security concerns it presents. This duality is at the heart of AI's story: while it offers revolutionary solutions and unprecedented efficiencies, it also poses challenges that require thoughtful and proactive management. My mission is to guide you through this intricate landscape with a balanced, comprehensive approach.

In this book, you will explore:
- Foundations of AI: Demystify the core concepts and tools that underpin artificial intelligence and machine learning, understanding their transformative potential in industries worldwide.
- Applications and Success Stories: Witness how AI has been successfully implemented to boost innovation, efficiency, and social good across various sectors.
- AI Security and Threats: Dive into real-world examples of AI vulnerabilities and learn best practices to secure systems against adversarial threats and data breaches.
- Governance and Ethics: Understand why ethical AI practices and governance frameworks are essential for promoting transparency, reducing bias, and building public trust.
- Future Trends and Leadership Strategies: Equip yourself with the knowledge of emerging AI trends and the skills necessary for effective human-AI collaboration.

This introduction is more than a preview; it's a manifesto for responsible leadership in the age of AI. True progress is not defined by technological breakthroughs alone, but by the integrity with which we wield these tools to improve human lives and society as a whole. I invite you to reflect on the dual nature of AI its power to innovate and its potential to disrupt and to consider your role in shaping its trajectory.

Before we delve into these topics, I would like to extend my heartfelt thanks to those who have been instrumental in this journey. To my colleagues at Kazma Technology and the dedicated team behind ChatWeft: your tireless work and unwavering commitment inspire me daily. To my friends, mentors, and the countless individuals who have supported and challenged me thank you for your insight and encouragement. Your belief in the pursuit of ethical, secure, and responsible AI has been my guiding light.

As you read, I encourage you to think critically, act responsibly, and lead with empathy. The age of AI is not just about machines or algorithms; it's about people. It's about how we, as stewards of technology, choose to harness it to create a future that is secure, ethical, and inclusive.

Welcome to The AI Compass. Your journey toward responsible, impactful AI leadership begins now.

Contents

Understanding and Demystifying AI

1. Demystifying AI and ML	2
2. Generative AI for Business Leaders	3
3. The Power of Generative AI	5
4. LLMs (Large Language Models)	7
5. AI & Key Tools	9
6. AI/ML Transforming Industries	10
7. AI/ML Trends and Predictions	11
8. Integrating Voice Capabilities with GPT	13
9. Using AI to Enhance Productivity	14
10. Transforming Customer Experience with AI	15

AI Applications and Success Stories

11. Real-World AI/ML Success Stories	17
12. AI/ML for Social Good	19
13. AI Tools to Boost Productivity	21
14. Essential Tools for AI/ML	23
15. AI-Powered Skills to Acquire for Career Advancement	25
16. The Future of Work: Human-AI Collaboration	26

Navigating AI Security

17. AI Security	28
18. Real-World Case Studies of AI Security Breaches	29
19. AI Security Threats and Solutions	31
20. AI Threat Detection and Response	33
21. Understanding Adversarial Machine Learning	34
22. AI Bias and Its Security Implications	36
23. Securing AI Models: Best Practices	37
24. Resources for Staying Informed on AI Security	38
25. AI in Crisis Management	39
26. Data Privacy and Protection in AI Systems	41
27. Edge AI	42
28. AI Risk Assessment Framework	44
29. Privacy Considerations in AI	50

AI Governance and Ethics

30. AI Governance and AI Ethics	49
31. The Role of Ethics in AI Governance	50
32. Ethics in AI Security	51
33. Responsible AI for Managers	52
34. Corporate Responsibility in AI	54
35. Combating AI Bias through Governance	55
36. AI Ethics and Bias	56
37. Key Principles of AI Governance	58
38. Key Principles of Effective AI Governance	60
39. Building an AI Governance Framework: A Step-by-Step Guide	61
40. AI Governance vs. Regulation: Know the Difference	62
41. How AI Governance Builds Trust with Users	64
42. AI Governance: Why It Matters	65
43. The Role of Governments in AI Governance	66
44. The Role of Stakeholders	67
45. Emerging Trends in AI Governance	69
46. Overcoming Challenges in AI Governance	70
E47. xplainable AI (XAI)	71
48. Ethical AI Design Principles	73
49. International Cooperation for AI Ethics	75
50. Global Regulatory Landscape	76

AI Ethics, Future Trends, and Final Thoughts

51. AI Ethics: Best Practices for Responsible AI Adoption	79
52. Companies Setting the Bar for AI Governance	80
53. Safe Cognitive and Sovereign AI Symposium	82
54. Future Trends in AI Governance	83
55. AI Talent War	85
56. AI/ML Trends and Predictions	86
57. AI-Powered Skills to Acquire for Career Advancement	88
58. AI/ML for Social Good	89

Real-World Examples and Case Studies

59. Real-World Case Studies	92

Understanding and Demystifying AI

Chapter-1

Demystifying AI and ML

Understanding Key Concepts and Real-World Applications

Artificial Intelligence (AI)

Artificial Intelligence (AI) refers to the simulation of human intelligence by machines, enabling them to perform tasks that typically require human cognition—like learning, problem-solving, and decision-making.

Machine Learning (ML)

Machine Learning (ML) is a subset of AI that allows systems to learn from data, identify patterns, and make decisions with minimal human intervention. Think of it as teaching machines to "learn" from experience.

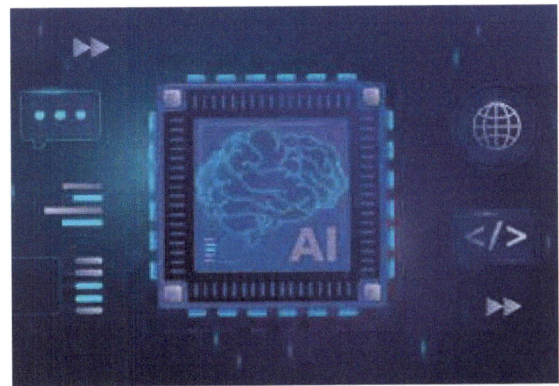

Deep Learning

Deep Learning is a more advanced form of Machine Learning, using neural networks with multiple layers to analyze complex data. It powers applications like voice assistants, facial recognition, and autonomous vehicles.

Neural Networks

Neural Networks are inspired by the human brain and consist of interconnected nodes (neurons). These networks process data through layers to identify patterns and improve accuracy over time.

AI is all around us! Here are some everyday examples:

- Personal Assistants: Siri, Alexa, Google Assistant
- Recommendation Systems: Netflix, Amazon
- Navigation: Google Maps, Waze
- Spam Filters: Gmail, Outlook

AI and ML are transforming industries across the board:

- Healthcare: Predictive diagnosis, personalized medicine
- Finance: Fraud detection, algorithmic trading
- Retail: Personalized shopping experiences
- Manufacturing: Predictive maintenance, automation

AI and ML are not just buzzwords—they're powerful tools reshaping the future. Understanding these technologies is the first step toward leveraging them in your business and everyday life. How do you see AI and ML impacting your industry?

GENERATIVE AI FOR BUSINESS LEADERS

Chapter-2

Generative AI for Business Leaders

Unlocking Innovation & Growth with AI

Generative AI refers to AI systems that can create new content, from text to images, code, and more. It's a powerful tool for driving innovation, enhancing productivity, and solving complex problems.

Generative AI is not just a tech trend; it's a game-changer in business. It can:

1. Automate content creation
2. Enhance product design
3. Personalize customer experiences
4. Drive business innovation

Key Benefits of Generative AI for Businesses:

- **Innovation at Scale:** Generate new ideas and concepts rapidly.
- **Operational Efficiency:** Automate repetitive tasks, freeing up time for strategic decisions.
- **Personalization:** Tailor products and services to individual customer needs.
- **Data-Driven Insights:** Enhance decision-making with AI-generated predictions and models.
- **Marketing & Content Creation:** Automate the creation of ads, blogs, and social media posts.
- **Product Design & Development:** Use AI to generate new product concepts or optimize existing ones.
- **Customer Service:** Deploy AI-generated chatbots for personalized customer interaction.
- **Financial Modeling:** Generate accurate predictions and optimize investment strategies.

The AI Compass: Security, Ethics, and Leadership

GENERATIVE AI FOR BUSINESS LEADERS

Challenge:
Ethical Concerns

Solution:
Develop guidelines for responsible AI use in content and decision-making.

Challenge:
Integration into Business Processes

Solution:
Start small with pilot projects and scale up as you gain confidence.

Challenge:
Quality Control

Solution:
Implement rigorous AI oversight and human-in-the-loop processes.

- **Educate Yourself:** Learn the fundamentals of generative AI.
- **Identify Use Cases:** Focus on areas where AI can have the most impact.
- **Collaborate with Experts:** Partner with AI specialists to develop and implement solutions.
- **Measure & Iterate:** Continuously measure results and refine your AI

Generative AI is more than a tool; it's a catalyst for transformation. Leaders who embrace it today will shape the businesses of tomorrow. How will you use generative AI to drive your business forward?

THE POWER OF GENERATIVE AI

Chapter-3

The Power of Generative AI

Discover How Generative AI is Transforming Industries by Creating New Content

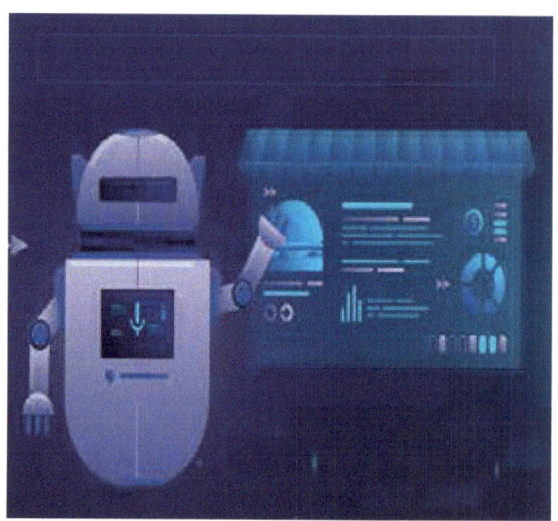

Generative AI

Generative AI refers to machine learning models that can create new content, such as text, images, and music. These models learn from existing data and use that knowledge to generate new, original content.

Popular Generative AI Models

- GANs (Generative Adversarial Networks)
- Transformers (e.g., GPT-4)
- VAEs (Variational Autoencoders)

GANs

GANs are a type of generative AI model where two neural networks—one generating data (the generator) and one evaluating it (the discriminator)—compete against each other to create realistic outputs.

Applications:

- Creating realistic images and videos
- Developing lifelike avatars for gaming and virtual environments
- Generating new art and design concepts

VAEs

VAEs are generative models that learn to encode data into a compressed form and then decode it back to generate new content. They are commonly used for generating variations of existing data.

Applications:

- Image generation and transformation
- Data augmentation for machine learning models
- Creating 3D models and virtual environments

THE POWER OF GENERATIVE AI

Generative AI

Generative AI models like GPT-4 can write articles, generate creative stories, and even code. By training on vast amounts of text data, these models can generate human-like text, making them valuable for content creation.

Applications:

- Automated content generation for blogs and articles
- AI-powered creative writing
- Code generation for software development

Generative AI

Generative AI can create stunning art, music compositions, and even design elements. Artists and creators are using AI as a tool to explore new forms of creativity, blending human input with machine-generated results.

Applications:

- AI-generated paintings and digital art
- Music composition and soundtracks
- Fashion and graphic design concepts

Generative AI

Generative AI is not just about art and text; it's transforming industries like healthcare, finance, and marketing. From creating synthetic medical data to designing innovative products, generative AI is revolutionizing the way businesses operate.

Applications:

- Synthetic data generation for medical research
- Designing new products in manufacturing
- Personalized marketing content creation

The possibilities for generative AI are endless, but it also comes with challenges. Ethical considerations, content authenticity, and responsible usage will be crucial as this technology continues to evolve. What future innovations will generative AI bring?

Chapter-4

What's the Buzz About LLMs?

Large Language Models (LLMs) are revolutionizing industries with their ability to understand and generate human-like text. But not all LLMs are the same. Let's explore different types of LLMs, compare their computing power, and discover how they're making life easier for everyone.

Exploring Different LLMs:

 GPT (Generative Pre-trained Transformer): Known for generating human-like text, widely used in creative content and chatbots.

 BERT (Bidirectional Encoder Representations from Transformers): Focuses on understanding context, ideal for sentiment analysis and Q&A.

 T5 (Text-To-Text Transfer Transformer): Versatile across many applications, converting tasks into text-to-text format.

Breaking Down LLMs

LLMs are advanced AI models trained on massive datasets to understand and generate language. They can perform tasks like language translation, summarization, and content creation. Popular examples include GPT, BERT, and T5.

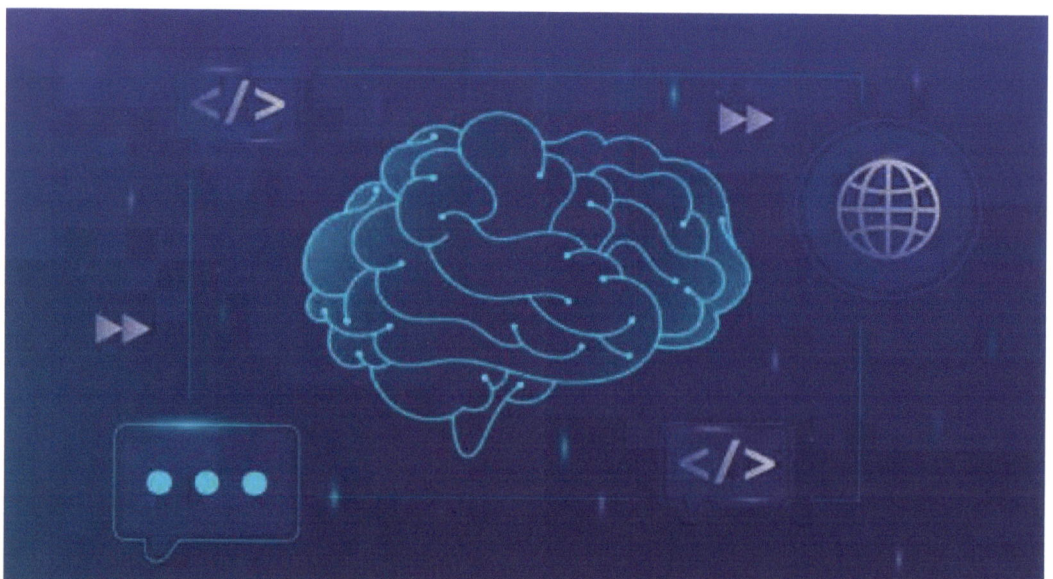

LLM'S

LLMs: Size & Computing Power:

- GPT-3: 175 billion parameters, requiring extensive computing resources, making it suitable for large-scale applications.

- BERT (Base): 110 million parameters, less resource-intensive but excels in nuanced text understanding.

- T5: Available in various sizes, from 60 million to 11 billion parameters, offering a balance between versatility and computing needs.

> **The Power Behind LLMs**
>
> LLMs require substantial computing power, especially for training and real-time applications. Larger models demand more GPUs and CPUs, leading to reliance on cloud-based AI infrastructure. The cost of scaling can be a significant challenge for businesses.

LLMs Simplifying Life:

- Healthcare: Assisting in diagnosis through NLP-powered medical record analysis.
- Personalization: They tailor experiences in real-time, such as product recommendations.
- Accessibility: Breaking down language barriers with real-time translation.

LLMs in Action Across Industries:

- Automation: LLMs power chatbots and automate repetitive tasks, saving time.
- Retail: Powering recommendation engines for personalized shopping experiences.
- Education: Enhancing personalized learning by generating study materials and tutoring.

What's Next for LLMs?

As LLMs evolve, they will continue to impact industries with even more powerful models. The future promises smarter AI that will tackle complex tasks, further simplifying human life and driving innovation.

Final Thoughts on LLMs

LLMs are transforming how we interact with technology. Their success relies on balancing powerful computing infrastructure with practical, value-adding applications. Are you ready to harness the potential of LLMs?

Explore More!

Dive deeper into how LLMs are shaping the future. [Insert article link].
Let's discuss how AI can empower your business. Share your thoughts in the comments!

AI & KEY TOOLS

Chapter-5

Unlocking the Power of AI and ML

Welcome to our series on AI and ML basics! Here, we'll cover the fundamentals of Artificial Intelligence and Machine Learning, and explore how they're transforming industries.

What is Artificial Intelligence?

AI refers to the development of computer systems that can perform tasks that typically require human intelligence, such as learning, problem-solving, and decision-making.

Types of Artificial Intelligence :

- Narrow or Weak AI
- General or Strong AI
- Super Intelligence

What is Machine Learning?

ML is a subset of AI that involves training algorithms to learn from data and make predictions or decisions without being explicitly programmed.

Types of Machine Learning :

- Supervised Learning
- Unsupervised Learning
- Reinforcement Learning

ML can be categorized into three types, each with its own approach to learning from data.

Real-World Applications of AI and ML

- Image and Speech Recognition
- Predictive Analytics
- Natural Language Processing
- Robotics

AI and ML are being used in various industries, from healthcare to finance, to drive innovation and efficiency.

Start Your AI and ML Journey

We hope this has has provided a solid foundation for understanding AI and ML basics. Stay tuned for more advanced topics and industry applications!

Good luck with your AI Journey!

Chapter-6

AI/ML Transforming Industries
Revolutionizing Sectors from Healthcare to Retail

AI/ML is enabling predictive diagnostics, personalized treatments, and even robot-assisted surgeries. From analyzing medical images to developing treatment plans, AI is improving healthcare outcomes.

- Benefits: Faster diagnosis, personalized care, and improved patient outcomes.
- Challenges: Data privacy, ethical concerns, and regulatory hurdles.

In finance, AI/ML is transforming risk management, fraud detection, and algorithmic trading. Financial institutions are leveraging these technologies to analyze large datasets, predict market trends, and prevent fraudulent activities.

- Benefits: Enhanced security, real-time risk assessment, and efficient trading.
- Challenges: High complexity, regulatory compliance, and potential biases.

AI/ML is streamlining manufacturing processes through predictive maintenance, quality control, and automation. Factories are using AI to reduce downtime, optimize production lines, and ensure high-quality output.

- Benefits: Reduced costs, minimized downtime, and increased efficiency.
- Challenges: High initial investment, workforce upskilling, and system integration.

Retailers are using AI/ML for personalized shopping experiences, dynamic pricing, and inventory management. From recommendation systems to AI chatbots, the technology is redefining customer engagement and operations.

- Benefits: Personalized marketing, optimized inventory, and improved customer satisfaction.
- Challenges: High inData accuracy, customer privacy, and maintaining relevance in a competitive market

Despite the benefits, AI/ML implementation faces challenges across industries:

- Data Privacy: Ensuring sensitive data is protected.
- Bias: Addressing biases in AI algorithms that can affect decisions.
- Regulation: Navigating complex legal frameworks and compliance issues.
- Workforce Impact: Balancing automation with the need for human jobs and upskilling.

The potential for AI/ML across industries is vast. As technology evolves, industries will see deeper integration of AI, leading to smarter, more efficient systems. Embracing this change while addressing the challenges is key to unlocking the full potential of AI/ML.

AI/ML is transforming industries and reshaping the future of business. Are you ready to embrace this revolution? How do you see AI/ML impacting your sector? Let's discuss!

Chapter-7

The Future of AI/ML: Trends and Predictions

Explore Emerging Trends Shaping the Future of AI/ML

Explainable AI (XAI): Making AI Transparent

One of the biggest challenges in AI today is its "black-box" nature, where even developers don't fully understand how AI models make decisions. Explainable AI (XAI) seeks to make AI systems more transparent and understandable, fostering trust in AI by explaining how decisions are made.

Why It Matters:

- Builds trust in AI systems
- Promotes ethical AI use
- Enables better decision-making with AI insights

Federated Learning: Decentralized AI Training

Federated learning allows AI models to be trained across multiple devices without the need to share sensitive data. This trend is gaining traction, particularly in industries like healthcare and finance, where data privacy is critical. The models learn collaboratively without compromising user privacy.

Why It Matters:

- Enhances data privacy
- Reduces risks associated with data breaches
- Enables collaborative learning across decentralized systems

AI in Edge Computing: Smarter Devices

AI is moving closer to where data is generated—on edge devices like smartphones, IoT devices, and drones. Edge AI reduces latency, increases efficiency, and enables real-time decision-making without relying on cloud connectivity. Industries like autonomous vehicles and smart cities are embracing this trend.

Why It Matters:

- Enables real-time processing and decision-making
- Powers intelligent IoT and autonomous systems

AI for Sustainability: Tackling Climate Change

AI is playing a crucial role in addressing climate change and environmental sustainability. From optimizing energy consumption to predicting natural disasters, AI models are being leveraged to solve complex environmental challenges, making industries greener and more sustainable.

Why It Matters:

- Reduces carbon footprints
- Optimizes resource usage
- Helps predict and mitigate climate disasters

AI/ML TRENDS AND PREDICTIONS

AI Democratization: Making AI Accessible

AI democratization refers to making AI technology accessible to everyone, not just tech giants. Tools like low-code/no-code platforms are enabling non-experts to build AI solutions, allowing small businesses and startups to leverage AI for innovation. This trend is creating new opportunities across industries.

Why It Matters:

- Broadens access to AI tools
- Spurs innovation across industries
- Empowers non-technical users to create AI solutions

Future Prediction: AI Co-Evolution with Humans

As AI continues to evolve, it will not replace humans but augment human capabilities. The future will see more collaboration between humans and AI, where AI handles repetitive tasks and humans focus on creativity, innovation, and emotional intelligence. AI will be our co-pilot in solving global challenges.

Why It Matters:

- AI complements human abilities
- Helps solve complex problems that require both AI and human intelligence
- Unlocks new opportunities for creativity and innovation

The future of AI/ML is bright, with emerging trends reshaping industries and society. As we move forward, staying informed about these trends and ethical considerations will be crucial. What are your thoughts on the future of AI/ML?

INTEGRATING VOICE CAPABILITIES WITH GPT

Chapter-8
Integrating Voice with GPT: The Future of AI Interaction

> **Key Benefits of Voice Integration:**
>
> 1. Enhanced User Engagement
> 2. Natural, Conversational Interfaces
> 3. Hands-Free Interactions

Discover how combining voice technology with GPT models can create seamless, interactive experiences. Here's a step-by-step guide to get you started!

Convert Voice to Text

Use services like Google Cloud Speech-to-Text, IBM Watson, or Microsoft Azure to transform spoken language into text. This is the first step in enabling voice interactions with GPT.

Process Text with GPT

Feed the converted text into OpenAI's GPT model. Generate intelligent responses based on the user's input. This step allows GPT to understand and respond to voice commands.

Convert Text Back to Voice

Use text-to-speech services like Google Cloud Text-to-Speech or Amazon Polly to convert GPT's response back into spoken language. This completes the voice interaction loop.

Integrate and Deploy

Combine the speech-to-text, GPT, and text-to-speech components in your application. Deploy it on a server or cloud platform to start providing voice-activated AI experiences.

Ready to Innovate?

Feel free to comment or DM me for guidance and advice on integrating voice with GPT. Let's explore the future of AI together!

Chapter-9

Unlocking Personal Productivity with AI/ML

Discover AI Tools and Techniques to Boost Efficiency and Automate Your Work

AI can automate repetitive tasks, streamline workflows, and provide intelligent insights, freeing up your time for higher-value activities. Whether you're a manager, entrepreneur, or professional, AI can help you achieve more in less time.

Key Benefits:

- Automate mundane tasks
- Improve decision-making with data-driven insights
- Enhance focus and efficiency

AI tools can handle repetitive tasks like scheduling, email sorting, and document organization. Platforms like *ZAPIER* and *IFTTT* connect apps and automate workflows, while AI-powered virtual assistants like *GOOGLE ASSISTANT* and *CORTANA* manage reminders and meetings.

Examples:

- Automate email responses with Gmail's Smart Reply
- Use AI to schedule meetings with tools like x.ai
- Set up task automation with *Zapier* or *IFTTT*

AI can analyze vast amounts of data to help you make more informed decisions. Tools like *WOLFRAM ALPHA* and *IBM WATSON* provide predictive analytics, helping you choose the best course of action based on data trends.

Examples:

- Use AI-powered analytics platforms like *Power BI* or *Tableau* for insights
- Get personalized recommendations with AI in apps like Netflix or Spotify
- Leverage AI for financial decision-making using apps like *Klarna*

Chapter-10

Revolutionize Customer Experience with AI

Discover how AI can enhance customer service, personalize experiences, and drive loyalty

1. 24/7 Support with AI Chatbots

- Instant responses
- Personalized solutions
- Reduced wait times
- Increased efficiency

2. Conversational Interfaces

- Voice assistants
- Text-based interfaces
- Multilingual support
- Hands-free experience

3. Anticipate Customer Needs

- Behavioral analysis
- Purchase history
- Real-time recommendations
- Proactive support

4. Segment Customers with AI

- Behavioral clustering
- Demographic analysis
- Preference profiling
- Targeted marketing

5. Tailored Experiences

- Content recommendations
- Customized offers
- Dynamic pricing
- Omnichannel engagement

6. Companies Leading the Way

- Amazon's Alexa
- Netflix's recommendations
- Starbucks' personalized offers
- American Express's AI-powered chatbots

7. Listen to Customer Feedback

- Emotion detection
- Sentiment analysis
- Net Promoter Score (NPS)
- Continuous improvement

8. Getting Started with AI-Powered Customer Experience

- Assess current infrastructure
- Identify AI opportunities
- Develop AI strategy
- Monitor and optimize

AI Applications and Success Stories

Chapter-11

Real-World AI/ML Success Stories
How AI/ML is Solving Complex Problems and Driving Innovation

Healthcare

AI is revolutionizing healthcare by improving diagnostics. For example, Google's AI algorithm achieved a 94.5% accuracy rate in detecting breast cancer in mammograms, surpassing human radiologists. AI's ability to analyze complex medical data enables faster and more accurate diagnoses, saving lives.

Key Benefits:

- Early disease detection
- Improved diagnostic accuracy
- Reduced human error

E-commerce

E-commerce giants like 'Amazon' use AI to personalize shopping experiences by analyzing customer data and predicting preferences. Amazon's recommendation engine, powered by machine learning, is responsible for 35% of its total sales. AI-driven personalization boosts customer satisfaction and drives revenue growth.

Key Benefits:

- Personalized recommendations
- Enhanced customer engagement
- Increased sales and loyalty

REAL-WORLD AI/ML SUCCESS STORIES

Bank & Financial Institution

Banks and financial institutions use AI/ML algorithms to detect and prevent fraudulent transactions. 'JP Morgan's' AI system, COiN, analyzes legal documents and transactions to identify fraud patterns, saving 360,000 hours of manual work annually. AI is improving security and efficiency in the finance sector.

Key Benefits:

- Real-time fraud detection
- Reduced manual workload
- Increased financial security

Siemens

Siemens uses AI in its manufacturing plants to optimize production and predict equipment failures. AI-powered predictive maintenance systems reduce downtime by up to 20%, ensuring smooth operations and increasing productivity. AI is transforming manufacturing by making processes more efficient.

Key Benefits:

- Predictive maintenance
- Reduced downtime
- Optimized production processes

Farmers

Farmers are using AI-powered tools to monitor crop health, optimize irrigation, and predict weather patterns. 'John Deere's' AI-driven machinery analyzes soil conditions and applies precise amounts of water and fertilizer, increasing crop yields by up to 15%. AI is helping farmers feed a growing world population.

Key Benefits:

- Optimized resource usage
- Sustainable farming practices
- Improved crop health and yield

DHL

'DHL' uses AI/ML to optimize its supply chain operations by predicting demand, optimizing delivery routes, and reducing fuel consumption. AI helps DHL achieve faster delivery times, lower costs, and improved customer satisfaction, making logistics more efficient and sustainable.

Key Benefits:

- Optimized delivery routes
- Faster delivery times
- Reduced operational costs

AI and ML continue to solve complex problems and create innovative solutions across industries. From healthcare to logistics, AI's impact is undeniable. What future success stories will AI/ML bring?

Chapter-12
AI/ML for Social Good
How AI/ML is Addressing Global Challenges and Creating a Positive Impact.

AI is transforming healthcare by improving diagnostics, treatment, and patient outcomes. For example, AI-driven tools can detect diseases like cancer in their early stages, enabling timely intervention and saving lives. AI-powered robotic surgeries are also making operations safer and more precise.

Impact:

- Early disease detection
- Precision medicine
- Improved patient outcomes

AI is breaking down barriers to education by creating personalized learning experiences for students. Tools like adaptive learning platforms adjust to students' needs, helping them learn at their own pace. AI is also enabling access to quality education for underserved communities worldwide.

Impact:

- Personalized learning paths
- Access to quality education
- Bridging the education gap

AI is helping to combat climate change by optimizing energy use, predicting natural disasters, and promoting sustainable practices. From reducing emissions to preserving biodiversity, AI is providing critical insights to help protect our planet.

Impact:

- Optimized energy consumption
- Predictive models for climate events
- Promoting sustainable practices

AI is enhancing social services by identifying areas of need, optimizing resource allocation, and improving access to essential services like housing and welfare. From food distribution to disaster relief, AI is empowering communities and making a tangible impact on people's lives.

Impact:

- Better resource distribution
- Optimized public service delivery
- Supporting vulnerable populations

AI/ML FOR SOCIAL GOOD

AI is being used to monitor and protect wildlife, track deforestation, and promote biodiversity. From using drones to track endangered species to satellite imagery analyzing environmental changes, AI is a powerful tool in conservation efforts.

Impact:

- Wildlife protection
- Forest conservation
- Promoting biodiversity

AI is helping humanitarian organizations respond faster and more effectively to crises. From mapping disaster zones using satellite imagery to predicting the spread of diseases in refugee camps, AI is saving lives by speeding up response efforts.

Impact:

- Faster disaster response
- Efficient resource allocation
- Saving lives in crisis situations

AI/ML has the power to address some of the world's most pressing challenges, from healthcare and education to climate action and crisis response. As we move forward, ensuring responsible AI development will be key to maximizing its positive impact.

Chapter-13

AI Tools to Boost Productivity

Discover 10 AI tools to streamline workflows, enhance efficiency, and save time

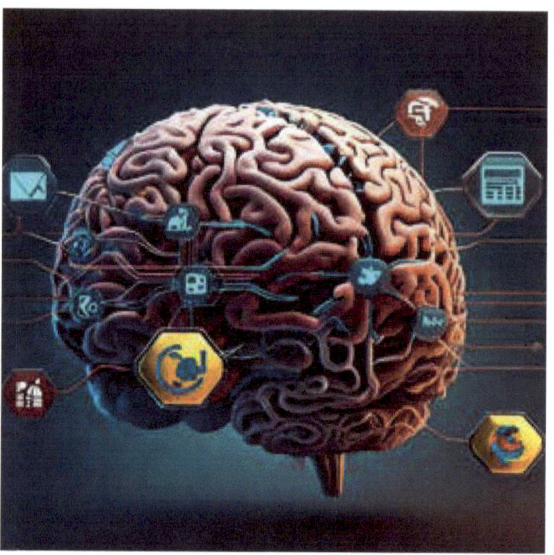

Refine Your Writing with Grammarly

AI-powered writing assistant for grammar, syntax, and style.

- Real-time grammar checking
- Suggested improvements
- Plagiarism detection

Schedule with Ease using Calendly

AI-powered scheduling tool for meetings and appointments

- Automated scheduling
- Time zone detection
- Integration with calendars

Organize Your Tasks with Trello

AI-powered project management tool for teams

- Visual boards
- Automated workflows
- Collaboration tools

Automate Meeting Notes with Spoke App

AI-powered meeting note-taking and summarization

- Real-time transcription
- Summarized notes
- Audio recording

AI TOOLS TO BOOST PRODUCTIVITY

Streamline Marketing with HubSpot
AI-powered marketing automation and CRM

- Lead generation
- Sales analytics
- Email automation

Boost Focus with Focus@Will
AI-powered music for productivity and concentration

- Customized playlists
- Reduced distractions
- Improved focus

Organize Your Thoughts with Evernote
AI-powered note-taking and organization

- Cross-platform syncing
- Handwriting recognition
- Image recognition

Manage Social Media with Hootsuite
AI-powered social media scheduling and analytics

- Automated posting
- Engagement tracking
- Content suggestions

Automate Workflows with Zapier
AI-powered workflow automation and integration

- Automated tasks
- Customized workflows
- App integrations

Manage Social Media with Hootsuite
AI-powered social media scheduling and analytics

- Automated posting
- Engagement tracking
- Content suggestions

Unlock Your Productivity Potential
Try these AI-powered tools to streamline your workflow and enhance efficiency

The AI Compass: Security, Ethics, and Leadership

ESSENTIAL TOOLS FOR AI/ML

Chapter-14
Essential Tools and Platforms for AI/ML
Unlock the Power of AI/ML with the Right Tools

TensorFlow: The Open-Source ML Framework
TensorFlow is a popular open-source machine learning framework developed by Google. It's widely used for building deep learning models and supports various tasks from image recognition to natural language processing.

Why Use It?

 Flexibility to deploy on different platforms (web, mobile, cloud).

 Extensive library for developing both research and production-level models.

PyTorch: Dynamic and Flexible ML Framework
PyTorch, developed by Facebook's AI Research lab, is known for its dynamic computation graph, making it ideal for research and development. It's particularly favored by researchers and academia for its ease of use and debugging.

Why Use It?

 Dynamic computation graph allows for easier experimentation.

 Seamless integration with Python, making it intuitive for developers.

Scikit-learn: The Go-To Library for Traditional ML
PyTorch, developed by Facebook's AI Research lab, is known for its dynamic computation graph, making it ideal for research and development. It's particularly favored by researchers and academia for its ease of use and debugging.

Why It Matters:

 Dynamic computation graph allows for easier experimentation.

 Seamless integration with Python, making it intuitive for developers.

Google Cloud AI Platform: Powering AI with Cloud
Google Cloud AI provides a suite of tools and services for developing, deploying, and managing AI models in the cloud. It's known for its scalability and integration with Google's robust infrastructure.

Why Use It?

 Access to pre-built models (e.g., Vision, Speech, Translation APIs).

 End-to-end model management, from data preparation to deployment.

ESSENTIAL TOOLS FOR AI/ML

AWS SageMaker: Build, Train, and Deploy ML Models

AWS SageMaker is Amazon's fully managed service that enables developers to build, train, and deploy machine learning models at scale. It provides all the tools necessary for every step of the ML lifecycle.

Why Use It?

 Integrated Jupyter notebooks for easy model development.

 Automatic model tuning and deployment options at scale.

Microsoft Azure AI: Democratizing AI Development

Microsoft Azure AI offers a suite of AI services and tools, enabling developers to build, train, and deploy AI models in the cloud. Azure is known for its enterprise-level security and integration with other Microsoft products.

Why Use It?

 Pre-built AI services for vision, speech, language, and decision-making.

 Highly secure and scalable platform ideal for enterprise use.

Selecting the right tools and platforms is crucial for success in AI/ML projects. Whether you're building deep learning models with TensorFlow or scaling up with Google Cloud AI, there's a tool for every need. What tools do you use for AI/ML development?

Chapter-15
Future-Proof Your Career with AI-Powered Skills
Stay ahead in the industry with in-demand AI skills.

1. Master ML Fundamentals
- Data preprocessing
- Algorithm selection
- Model training
- Deployment

2. Unlock NLP Potential
- Text analysis
- Language modeling
- Sentiment analysis
- Chatbots

3. Tell Stories with Data
- Data wrangling
- Statistical analysis
- Visualization tools
- Insight generation

4. Ensure Responsible AI
- Bias detection
- Transparency
- Fairness analysis
- Regulatory compliance

5. Dive into DL and Neural Networks
- Convolutional neural networks (CNNs)
- Generative adversarial networks (GANs)
- Recurrent neural networks (RNNs)
- Transfer learning

6. Transforming Industries
- Healthcare: predictive analytics
- Marketing: personalized recommendations
- Finance: risk analysis

7. Unlock New Career Opportunities
- AI engineer
- Business analyst
- Data scientist
- AI researcher

8. Develop Your AI Skills
- Online courses (Coursera, edX)
- Books and research papers
- Certifications (Google, Microsoft)
- Professional networks

Chapter-16
Unlocking Human Potential with AI Collaboration

Explore the benefits and challenges of human-AI collaboration.

1. Augmenting Human Capabilities
- Enhanced productivity
- Increased innovation
- Improved accuracy
- Personalized customer experiences

2. Addressing the Challenges
- Job displacement concerns
- Data quality and security
- Bias and ethics
- Change management

3. Integrating AI in the Workforce
- Start with automation of repetitive tasks
- Foster a culture of innovation
- Upskill and reskill employees
- Establish clear AI governance

4. Exploring Collaboration Models
- Human-in-the-loop (HITL)
- Human-with-the-loop (HWTL)
- Human-over-the-loop (HOTL)

5. Transforming Industries
- Healthcare: AI-assisted diagnosis
- Customer Service: AI-powered chatbots
- Finance: AI-driven risk analysis

6. Developing Essential Skills
- Data literacy
- Critical thinking
- AI fluency
- Emotional intelligence

7. Assess Your AI Readiness
- Technology infrastructure
- Talent acquisition
- Data preparedness
- Change management

8. Success Stories
- Microsoft's AI-powered customer service
- Google's AI-assisted healthcare
- IBM's AI-driven innovation

Navigating AI Security

AI SECURITY

Chapter-17

The Importance of AI Security

An overview of why AI security matters and its impact on businesses and society.

- AI security involves protecting AI systems from threats, vulnerabilities, and malicious attacks. As AI technologies grow, ensuring their security is crucial to maintain trust and functionality.

- AI systems are increasingly integrated into critical sectors like healthcare, finance, and transportation. A breach can lead to severe consequences, including financial loss, data leaks, and compromised safety.

- For businesses, AI security is essential for protecting intellectual property, customer data, and maintaining competitive advantage. Breaches can result in costly downtime and damage to reputation.

- AI systems can influence societal norms and behaviors. Insecure AI can lead to biased decision-making and ethical concerns, impacting social justice and equality.

- Examples of AI security breaches (e.g., data poisoning in self-driving cars) highlight the need for robust security measures. Such breaches can endanger lives and public trust in technology.

- Threats include adversarial attacks, data poisoning, and model inversion. Understanding these threats is the first step toward developing effective security strategies.

- Implementing best practices like robust data validation, continuous monitoring, and regular updates can significantly enhance AI security.

- Ethical considerations in AI security are vital. Organizations must prioritize transparency, accountability, and fairness in AI development to foster public trust.

- As AI technology evolves, so do the threats. Investing in AI security is essential for future innovation, resilience, and protecting societal interests.

Stay informed and proactive about AI security. Join the conversation, share knowledge, and contribute to making AI technologies safe for everyone.

REAL-WORLD CASE STUDIES

Chapter-18

Real-World Case Studies in AI Governance

Lessons from Successful Frameworks Around the Globe

We will explore key lessons learned from various organizations and countries

Canada's AI Framework

Canada's Directive on Automated Decision-Making ensures transparency and accountability. Key elements include risk assessments and clear communication about AI decisions.

Lessons Learned:

- Clear guidelines foster trust.
- Regular audits can mitigate risks.
- Engage stakeholders early in the process.

European Union AI Act

The EU's AI Act aims to create a comprehensive regulatory framework for AI. It categorizes AI applications based on risk and imposes strict obligations on high-risk AI systems.

Lessons Learned:

- Proactive regulation is key to innovation.
- Risk-based approach promotes responsible use.
- Collaboration among member states enhances effectiveness.

REAL-WORLD CASE STUDIES

Microsoft's AI Principles

Microsoft's AI governance framework focuses on fairness, reliability, privacy, and inclusivity. They emphasize ethical AI development and provide resources for responsible AI usage.

Lessons Learned:

- Clear ethical guidelines enhance corporate responsibility.
- Transparency builds customer trust.
- Employee training on AI ethics is essential.

Singapore's Smart Nation Initiative

Singapore promotes AI governance through its Smart Nation initiative, focusing on responsible AI deployment. They incorporate public feedback in AI system designs to ensure societal acceptance.

Lessons Learned:

- Public engagement leads to better outcomes.
- Collaboration between public and private sectors enhances innovation.
- Regular updates based on feedback are crucial.

These case studies highlight the importance of effective AI governance.

By learning from successful frameworks, organizations can foster trust and responsible AI use.

What are your thoughts on these case studies?

Share your experiences or insights on AI governance in the comments!

Chapter-19

AI Security Threats and Solutions
Identifying Risks and Effective Strategies to Combat Them

As AI systems become more prevalent, security threats are also evolving. Understanding these threats is essential to protect AI applications and their data.

Common AI Security Threats:
Key security threats facing AI systems include:

- Adversarial Attacks: Manipulating inputs to deceive AI models.
- Data Poisoning: Introducing malicious data to corrupt training datasets.
- Model Theft: Unauthorized access to replicate or steal AI models.

Adversarial Attacks:
- Adversarial attacks involve slight modifications to inputs that can mislead AI systems.
- Example: Changing a few pixels in an image can cause misclassification.

Data Poisoning:
- Data poisoning attacks aim to corrupt the training process of AI models.
- Attackers inject misleading data to skew model predictions.

Model Theft:
- Model theft occurs when unauthorized entities replicate AI models.
- This can lead to intellectual property theft and misuse of proprietary technology.

Effective Solutions for Adversarial Attacks:
- Adversarial Training: Train models with adversarial examples to improve robustness.
- Input Validation: Implement thorough validation techniques to identify suspicious inputs.

AI SECURITY THREATS AND SOLUTIONS

Mitigating Data Poisoning:

- Data Integrity Checks: Regularly audit and verify training datasets.
- Robust Data Selection: Use diverse and representative datasets to minimize susceptibility.

Protecting Against Model Theft:

- Access Controls: Implement strict access permissions to limit who can access models.
- Watermarking: Embed invisible watermarks in models to deter unauthorized usage.

Importance of Regular Security Audits:

- Regular security audits are essential for identifying vulnerabilities in AI systems.
- Conduct audits to assess threat landscapes and ensure compliance with security standards.

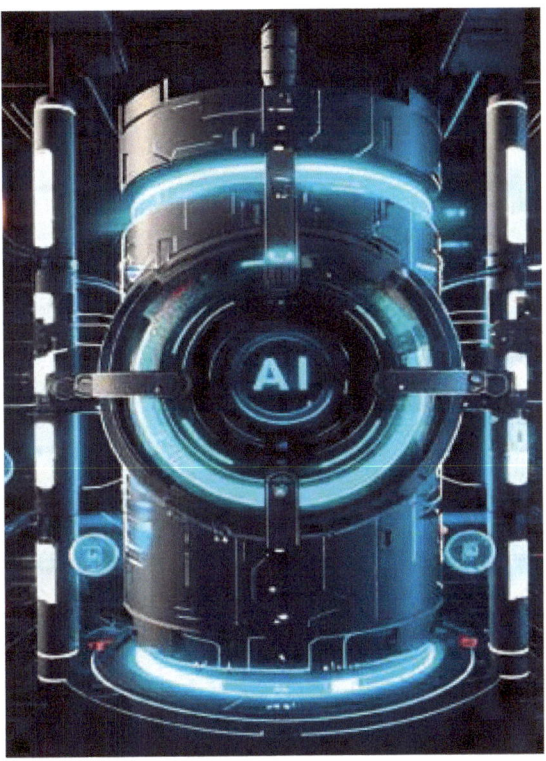

Addressing security threats in AI is critical for the integrity and trustworthiness of these systems. By implementing robust security measures, we can protect AI technologies and their applications.

What security measures do you implement for your AI systems?

Share your experiences and insights in the comments!

Chapter-20

AI Threat Detection and Response

AI threats refer to malicious activities that exploit vulnerabilities in AI systems, leading to potential security breaches.

- Common AI-specific threats include data poisoning, adversarial attacks, model inversion, and bias exploitation.
- Data poisoning occurs when attackers inject malicious data into training datasets, skewing AI outcomes.
- Adversarial attacks involve manipulating input data to deceive AI models, causing incorrect predictions.
- Model inversion allows attackers to extract sensitive information from AI models by querying them.
- Attackers can exploit AI bias to manipulate decisions and outcomes, undermining trust in AI systems.
- Effective detection techniques include anomaly detection, adversarial training, and robust model evaluations.
- Anomaly detection identifies unusual patterns in data that may indicate potential threats to AI systems.
- Adversarial training involves exposing AI models to adversarial examples during training to enhance robustness.

Response strategies include incident response plans, patch management, and continuous monitoring.

Chapter-21

Understanding Adversarial Machine Learning

A deep dive into how adversarial attacks work, examples, and mitigation strategies.

"Adversarial machine learning focuses on the study of techniques used to deceive AI models. These techniques exploit vulnerabilities in machine learning algorithms to manipulate their outputs."

Adversarial attacks involve adding subtle perturbations to input data that are imperceptible to humans but can drastically change the model's predictions. This can lead to misclassifications or incorrect outputs.

Types of Adversarial Attacks:

- Evasion Attacks: Altering input data during inference to mislead the model.
- Poisoning Attacks: Injecting harmful data into the training set to corrupt the model.
- Model Inversion Attacks: Extracting sensitive information from the model.

Real-World Examples of Adversarial Attacks:

- Image Recognition: In 2018, researchers successfully fooled an AI image classifier to misidentify a turtle as a rifle using adversarial noise.
- Autonomous Vehicles: Attacks on traffic signs can mislead self-driving cars, endangering safety.

Adversarial attacks can have severe consequences, including:

- Compromised safety in autonomous systems.
- Financial losses in businesses relying on AI for decision-making.
- Erosion of public trust in AI technologies.

UNDERSTANDING ADVERSARIAL MACHINE LEARNING

Mitigation Strategies:

- Adversarial Training: Training models on adversarial examples to improve robustness.
- Defensive Distillation: Reducing model sensitivity to input changes.
- Input Preprocessing: Filtering inputs to remove potential adversarial noise.

Developers can enhance AI security by:

- Regularly testing models against adversarial examples.
- Keeping abreast of the latest research on adversarial machine learning.
- Collaborating with security experts to understand vulnerabilities.

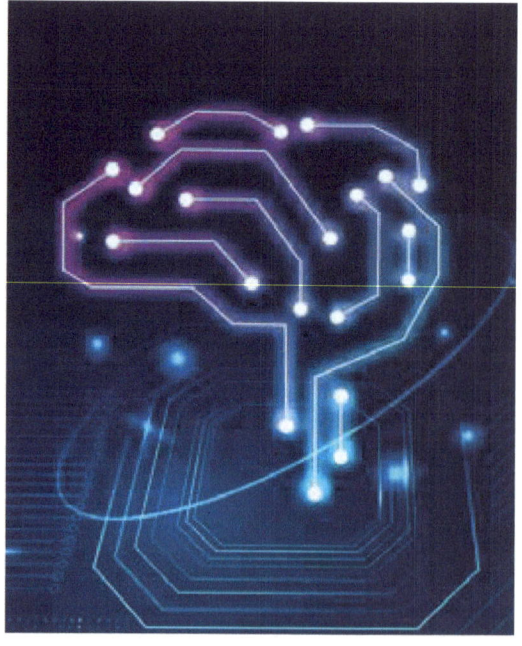

> *As AI technology advances, so will the sophistication of adversarial attacks. Ongoing research is crucial to developing more robust models and improving security in AI systems.*

Stay informed about adversarial machine learning and its implications. Share knowledge, collaborate on research, and contribute to building safer AI systems.

AI BIAS AND ITS SECURITY IMPLICATIONS

Chapter-22

AI Bias and Its Security Implications

What is AI Bias? It occurs when algorithms produce unfair outcomes due to prejudiced training data or flawed design.

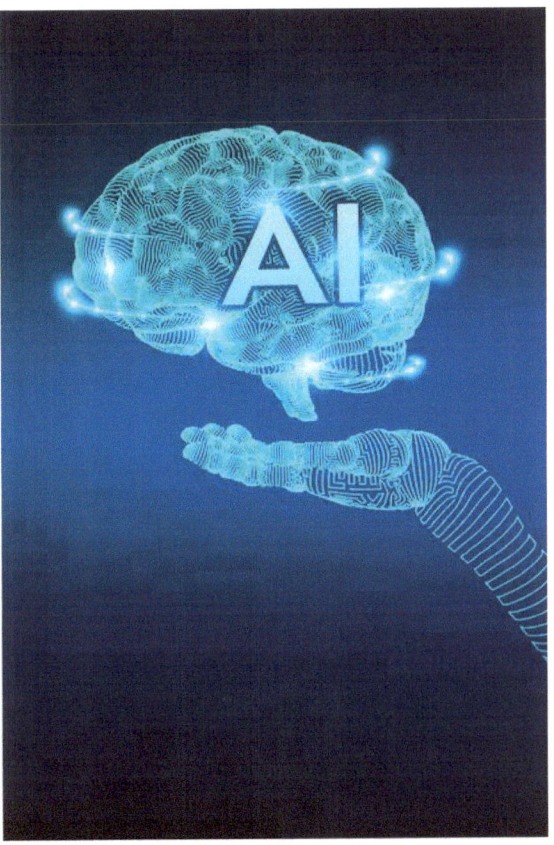

- Data bias arises from training datasets reflecting historical prejudices, leading to skewed AI outcomes.

- Algorithmic bias happens when algorithms favor certain groups or outcomes based on their design.

- Bias creates predictable AI behavior, making systems vulnerable to exploitation by malicious actors.

- Biased AI systems can disproportionately impact marginalized groups, leading to systemic discrimination

- Organizations using biased AI risk backlash and loss of public trust, leading to financial and reputational harm.

- Deployment of biased AI systems can lead to legal repercussions and regulatory scrutiny.

- Strategies to combat AI bias include using diverse datasets, bias detection tools, and transparent algorithms.

- Implementing AI ethics boards and governance frameworks ensures accountability and promotes ethical AI usage.

Join the conversation on AI bias and its implications. How can we work together to create a fairer future for AI?

Chapter-23

Securing AI Models: Best Practices

Tips for developing robust AI models, including secure coding practices and regular audits.

Securing AI models is essential to protect against adversarial attacks, data breaches, and model exploitation. Robust security practices ensure the reliability and trustworthiness of AI systems.

- Utilize version control systems (like Git) to track changes in code, datasets, and model configurations.
  This allows for better collaboration and easy rollback to previous versions if vulnerabilities are discovered.

- Regularly audit your AI models for vulnerabilities and compliance with security standards. This includes reviewing code, datasets, and model performance to identify potential weaknesses.

- Restrict access to your AI models and training data based on roles. Use authentication and authorization mechanisms to ensure only authorized personnel can interact with sensitive components.

- Encrypt sensitive data both in transit and at rest. This protects the integrity and confidentiality of the data used to train your AI models and ensures it remains secure from unauthorized access.

- Continuously monitor your AI models in production for unusual behavior or performance drops. Set up alerts for potential security incidents, allowing for quick responses to threats.

- Encourage a culture of security awareness within your development team. Provide training on security best practices, potential threats, and how to mitigate risks associated with AI systems.

AI security is an evolving field. Stay updated on the latest trends, research, and tools to adapt your practices and ensure the ongoing security of your AI models.

- Input Validation: Always validate and sanitize inputs to prevent malicious data from entering your models.

- Error Handling: Implement comprehensive error handling to prevent information leakage.

RESOURCES FOR STAYING INFORMED ON AI SECURITY

Chapter-24

Resources for Staying Informed on AI Security

Staying informed about AI security is crucial for professionals and organizations to mitigate risks and adapt to evolving threats.

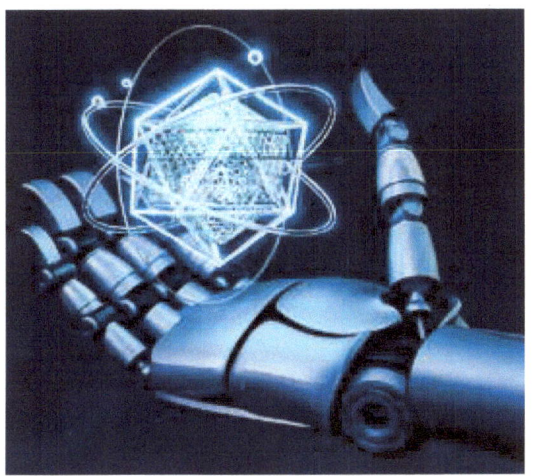

> *Artificial Intelligence: A Guide to Intelligent Systems'* by Michael Negnevitsky.
>
> *Weapons of Math Destruction'* by Cathy O'Neil.
>
> *AI Superpowers: China, Silicon Valley, and the New World Order'* by Kai-Fu Lee.

- Check out platforms like Coursera and edX for courses on AI security, ethics, and best practices.
- AI Now Institute - Research and insights on AI's social implications, including security.
- OpenAI Blog - Updates on AI research, ethical considerations, and security practices.
- Partnership on AI - A coalition dedicated to responsible AI development and safety.
- IEEE Global Initiative on Ethics of Autonomous and Intelligent Systems - Promotes ethical AI and security practices.
- Stay updated with journals like 'Artificial Intelligence,' 'AI & Society,' and 'Journal of AI Research' for cutting-edge research.

Join online forums and communities like AI Security Slack and Reddit's r/MachineLearning for discussions and insights.

Utilizing these resources will help you stay informed and proactive in addressing AI security challenges. What resources do you rely on for AI security knowledge? Share your recommendations in the comments!

Chapter-25
AI in Crisis Management
Ethical Considerations and Governance Frameworks

AI has transformative potential in managing crises like natural disasters and public health emergencies. However, ethical considerations and governance frameworks are critical to ensure responsible use.

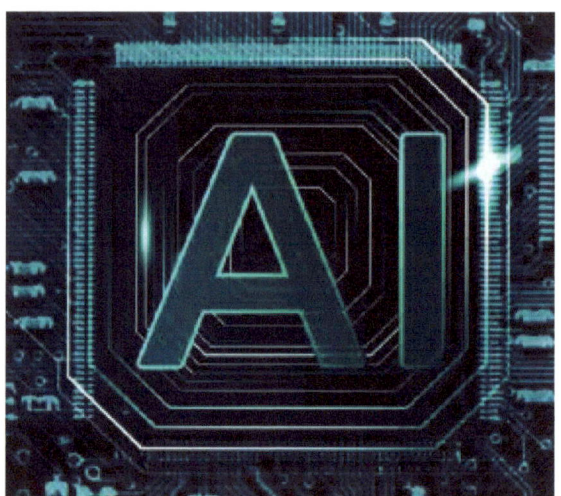

Importance of Ethics in Crisis Situations:
In crises, ethical considerations become even more crucial.

- How do we ensure equitable access to AI resources?
- What are the implications of AI decisions on vulnerable populations?
- How do we maintain transparency in AI-driven responses?

Governance Frameworks:
Effective governance frameworks are essential for guiding AI use in crises.

- Clear policies and guidelines for AI deployment.
- Mechanisms for oversight and accountability.
- Engagement with stakeholders, including communities affected by crises.

Data Privacy and Security:
Protecting data privacy and security is paramount in crisis management.

- Ensuring informed consent for data collection.
- Implementing robust cybersecurity measures.
- Maintaining data integrity while sharing information.

AI IN CRISIS MANAGEMENT

Bias and Fairness:

AI systems must be designed to avoid bias, especially in crisis situations.

- Regularly audit algorithms for fairness.
- Use diverse datasets representing all affected communities.
- Involve community representatives in AI development.

Accountability in AI Decisions:

Clear accountability is essential for AI-driven decisions during crises.

- Define who is responsible for AI actions.
- Implement feedback loops to monitor outcomes.
- Create avenues for redress when AI systems cause harm.

Collaboration Among Stakeholders:

Collaboration between various stakeholders enhances the effectiveness of AI in crises.

- Government agencies
- NGOs and community organizations

Transparency and Public Trust:

Transparency in AI operations fosters public trust, crucial during crises.

- Communicate clearly about AI capabilities and limitations.
- Share data and methodologies with the public.
- Regularly update communities on AI-driven decisions.

AI has the potential to greatly enhance crisis management, but it must be used ethically. By prioritizing governance frameworks, we can ensure that AI serves the best interests of all, especially during critical times.

What ethical considerations do you believe are crucial for AI in crisis management?

Share your thoughts and insights in the comments!

Chapter-26

Data Privacy and Protection in AI Systems

Exploring the importance of data privacy and regulations like GDPR in the context of AI.

Data privacy is crucial in AI systems as these technologies often rely on large datasets containing sensitive personal information. Protecting this data fosters trust and ensures compliance with regulations.

AI systems analyze vast amounts of data to learn patterns and make predictions. This often involves personal data, making it essential to handle such information responsibly and ethically. The General Data Protection Regulation (GDPR) is a comprehensive data privacy law in the EU that mandates how organizations should handle personal data, giving individuals more control over their information.

Key GDPR Principles Relevant to AI

- Data Minimization: Collect only the data necessary for a specific purpose.
- Purpose Limitation: Use personal data only for the intended purpose.
- Transparency: Clearly inform individuals about data collection and usage.

Failure to comply with data privacy regulations like GDPR can result in significant penalties, including hefty fines and reputational damage, which can affect business operations.

Best Practices for Data Privacy in AI

- Data Encryption: Protect data both at rest and in transit.
- Anonymization: Remove personally identifiable information from datasets.
- Regular Audits: Conduct audits to ensure compliance and identify vulnerabilities.

GDPR grants individuals rights regarding their data, including:

- Right to access
- Right to rectify
- Right to erasure (right to be forgotten)

Organizations must prioritize data privacy by implementing robust policies, training staff, and creating a culture of data protection to build trust with their users and comply with regulations.

As AI technology evolves, so do data privacy challenges. Expect increased regulations and technological advancements focused on enhancing data protection and user privacy.

Data privacy is everyone's responsibility. Stay informed about regulations like GDPR and share best practices to protect personal data in AI systems.

EDGE AI

Chapter-27

What is Edge AI?

Edge AI refers to the deployment of AI algorithms and models directly on edge devices, such as smartphones, IoT devices, and sensors, rather than relying on cloud-based processing.

Why Edge AI is Important?

Edge AI reduces latency, enhances privacy, minimizes bandwidth usage, and allows real-time decision-making at the device level.

Key Benefits :

- Low Latency: Faster response times.
- Privacy: Data processed locally, reducing exposure.
- Bandwidth Efficiency: Less data sent to the cloud.
- Reliability: Operates independently of network connectivity.

Applications of Edge AI :

- Smart Homes: Intelligent devices and voice assistants.
- Healthcare: Wearable devices for monitoring and diagnostics.
- Autonomous Vehicles: Real-time processing for navigation and safety.
- Retail: Smart cameras for inventory and customer insights.

Edge AI vs. Cloud AI:

- Edge AI: Processes data locally, reduces latency, enhances privacy.
- Cloud AI: Centralized processing, requires internet, potentially higher latency.

EDGE AI

Technologies Behind Edge AI:

- AI Chips: Specialized processors for edge devices.
- Edge Servers: Local servers that handle data processing.
- Software Frameworks: Tools and libraries for developing edge AI applications.

Challenges:

- Resource Constraints: Limited processing power and memory.
- Security: Ensuring data protection on edge devices.
- Scalability: Managing and updating numerous edge devices.

> ### The Future of Edge AI
> Edge AI is expected to evolve with advancements in AI hardware, increased adoption across industries, and enhanced security protocols, driving innovation in real-time applications.

Summary:

Edge AI brings AI capabilities directly to devices, offering benefits like low latency, enhanced privacy, and operational efficiency, while presenting challenges that are being addressed through technological advancements.

Explore Edge AI

Interested in implementing Edge AI in your projects? Connect with us or visit our website to learn more about how Edge AI can transform your solutions.

AI RISK ASSESSMENT FRAMEWORK

Chapter-28

AI Risk Assessment Framework
A Visual Guide to Identifying and Mitigating Risks in AI Projects

Introduction to AI Risk Assessment:

- Risk assessment is a critical step in AI project development.
- It involves identifying potential risks and implementing strategies to mitigate them, ensuring responsible AI deployment.

Identify Project Scope:

- Define the objectives, scope, and stakeholders of the AI project.
- Understanding the context is essential for accurate risk identification.

Identify Potential Risks:

Conduct a thorough analysis to identify risks, including-

- Data privacy risks
- Algorithmic bias
- Security vulnerabilities
- Regulatory compliance issues

AI RISK ASSESSMENT FRAMEWORK

Assess Risk Impact and Likelihood:

- Evaluate the impact and likelihood of each identified risk.
- Use a risk matrix to categorize risks as low, medium, or high.

Develop Mitigation Strategies:

For high-priority risks, develop targeted mitigation strategies, such as-

- Implementing data anonymization techniques
- Conducting regular audits for bias
- Enhancing cybersecurity measures

Assign Responsibilities:

- Designate team members responsible for monitoring and managing each risk.
- Clear accountability is essential for effective risk management.

Monitor and Review:

- Establish a process for continuous monitoring and review of risks.
- Regularly update risk assessments and mitigation strategies as the project evolves.

Document and Communicate:

- Document all findings, assessments, and strategies.
- Ensure transparent communication with stakeholders about risk management efforts.
- A robust AI risk assessment framework is vital for responsible AI development.
- By proactively identifying and mitigating risks, organizations can enhance trust and accountability in AI systems.

How does your organization approach AI risk assessment?

Share your thoughts or experiences in the comments!

Chapter-29
Privacy Considerations in AI
Ethical Implications and Best Practices for Data Handling

Introduction to Privacy in AI

- Data privacy is a critical concern in AI applications.
- As AI systems increasingly rely on personal data, understanding privacy implications is essential for ethical development.

Ethical Implications of Data Privacy

Ethical implications of data privacy in AI include:

- Informed consent: Are users fully aware of how their data will be used?
- Data ownership: Who owns the data collected by AI systems?
- Accountability: How can developers be held responsible for data misuse?

Best Practices for Data Handling

Implementing best practices for data handling is crucial for maintaining privacy.

- Minimize data collection: Collect only what is necessary.
- Anonymize data: Remove personally identifiable information (PII) when possible.
- Encrypt sensitive data: Protect data at rest and in transit.

User Consent

Obtaining user consent is vital in AI applications.

- Clarity: Use plain language to explain data usage.
- Granularity: Allow users to choose what data they share.
- Revocation: Provide an easy way for users to withdraw consent.

Transparency in Data Use

Transparency is key to building trust with users.

- Clearly communicate data practices.
- Share how data informs AI decisions.
- Regularly update users about changes in data policies.

PRIVACY CONSIDERATIONS IN AI

Data Security Measures

Implementing strong data security measures is essential.

- Conduct regular security audits.
- Train employees on data protection.
- Use multi-factor authentication for access control.

The Role of Regulations

Regulations play a vital role in safeguarding data privacy.

- General Data Protection Regulation (GDPR)
- California Consumer Privacy Act (CCPA)
- Other local data protection laws

Challenges in Privacy Management

Common challenges in managing privacy in AI include:

- Balancing innovation with privacy rights.
- Navigating complex regulatory landscapes.
- Addressing public skepticism about data usage.

Future Directions in AI Privacy

The future of AI privacy involves:

- Evolving technologies for better data protection.
- Greater emphasis on ethical AI frameworks.
- Increased collaboration between stakeholders for best practices.

Ethical data privacy practices are essential for responsible AI development.

By prioritizing user consent, transparency, and data security, we can foster trust and innovation.as a whole.

How do you ensure data privacy in your AI projects?

Share your thoughts or experiences in the comments!

AI Governance and Ethics

AI GOVERNANCE AND AI ETHICS

Chapter-30

AI Governance and AI Ethics

As AI continues to evolve, ensuring its responsible use becomes crucial. AI governance and AI ethics provide a framework for accountability, transparency, and fairness.

AI governance is a set of policies, regulations, and standards to guide the development, deployment, and monitoring of AI systems.

- AI ethics focuses on ensuring that AI systems respect human rights, fairness, and social good. Ethical AI avoids biases and promotes fairness.
- AI faces ethical challenges like bias, discrimination, lack of transparency, and decision-making without accountability.
- Bias in AI systems can lead to unfair outcomes. Ensuring fairness requires eliminating bias in data and algorithms.
- Transparency is key in AI governance. Users and stakeholders need to understand how decisions are made by AI systems.

The pillars of AI governance include:

1. Transparency
2. Inclusivity
3. Accountability
4. Fairness and Safety

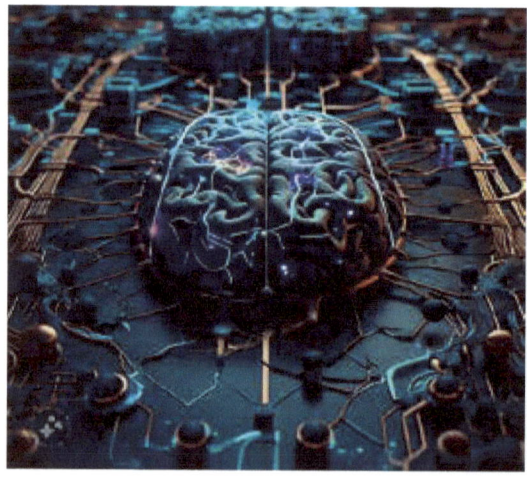

Accountability ensures that there are clear, responsible parties for AI decisions and outcomes. AI systems should not function in a vacuum.

Building ethical AI requires collaboration between governments, businesses, and civil society. We need diverse perspectives to ensure AI serves everyone.

Shape the future of AI! Get involved in discussions on AI governance and ethics. Let's build AI systems we can trust.

The AI Compass: Security, Ethics, and Leadership

Chapter-31

The Role of Ethics in AI Governance

Ethics play a vital role in shaping how we develop and deploy AI responsibly. Let's explore key ethical considerations!

- AI technologies can greatly benefit society, but ethical considerations ensure they do so without harming individuals or communities. Here's how ethics fit into AI governance.

- Respecting data privacy is crucial. Users should know how their data is collected, used, and stored. Ethical AI systems prioritize protecting personal information.

- Informed consent means users must understand what they are agreeing to when their data is used. Clear communication is key to ethical AI practices.

- Bias in AI can lead to unfair treatment. Ethical AI governance focuses on identifying and minimizing biases to ensure fairness for all users.

- Organizations must be accountable for their AI systems. If an AI makes a mistake, there should be clear processes to address it and make corrections.

- Transparency in AI processes allows users to see how decisions are made. Ethical AI should be understandable and accessible to everyone.

- Ethical AI also considers environmental impact. Sustainable AI practices minimize resource consumption and promote eco-friendly solutions.

- Incorporating ethics into AI governance is not just about compliance; it's about building trust, ensuring fairness, and creating a positive impact.

Ethics are at the heart of responsible AI governance. How do you ensure ethical practices in your AI projects?

Join the conversation and follow us for more insights!

Chapter-32

Ethics in AI Security

Ethics in AI refers to the principles guiding the development and deployment of AI technologies to ensure fairness, transparency, and accountability.

- Implementing ethical frameworks helps developers address moral dilemmas and make responsible decisions throughout the AI lifecycle.

- Transparency allows stakeholders to understand how AI systems make decisions, fostering trust and accountability.

- Ethically responsible AI includes actively addressing and mitigating bias to ensure fair outcomes for all users.

- Establishing AI ethics boards can provide guidance and oversight in the development and deployment of AI technologies.

- Unethical AI practices can lead to security vulnerabilities, misuse of data, and discrimination, undermining public trust.

- Ethical AI development prioritizes data privacy, ensuring user data is collected, stored, and used responsibly.

- Integrating ethical practices into security protocols ensures that AI systems are designed to protect users' rights and promote safety.

- Compliance with regulations like GDPR and CCPA is essential for ethical AI practices, ensuring data protection and user rights.

Organizations must provide continuous ethical training to developers and stakeholders to promote a culture of ethical AI.

What ethical considerations does your organization prioritize in AI development? Join the conversation and share your insights!

RESPONSIBLE AI FOR MANAGERS

Chapter-33

Responsible AI for Managers

Driving Ethical AI Practices for Sustainable Growth

As AI adoption increases, so do the ethical challenges. Responsible AI ensures fairness, transparency, and accountability, building trust with customers and stakeholders.

Key Pillars of Responsible AI

- Fairness – Avoid bias and ensure equity in AI decision-making.
- Transparency – Make AI processes understandable and explainable.
- Fairness – Avoid bias and ensure equity in AI decision-making.
- Transparency – Make AI processes understandable and explainable.

> *Managers play a critical role in AI governance. By ensuring responsible AI practices, they can:*
>
> *1. Mitigate risks*
> *2. Improve decision-making*
> *3. Enhance brand reputation*

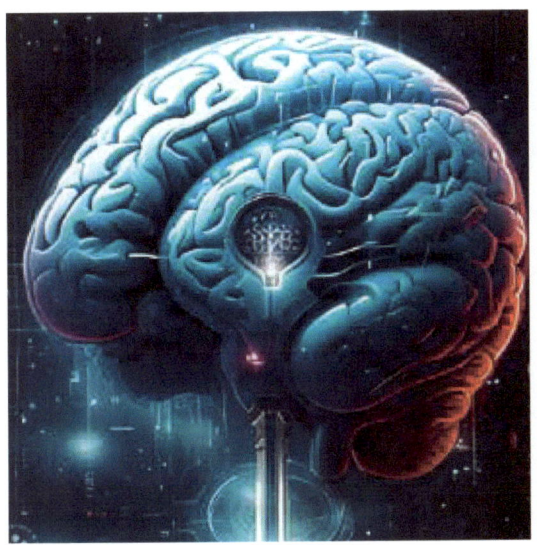

- Establish Guidelines: Define ethical AI standards for your team.
- Foster Collaboration: Work with data scientists, ethicists, and legal teams.
- Continuous Learning: Stay updated on AI trends and best practices.

RESPONSIBLE AI FOR MANAGERS

Challenge:
Bias in AI algorithms

Solution:
Implement bias detection tools and diverse datasets.

Challenge:
Lack of transparency

Solution:
Prioritize explainable AI techniques.

By promoting responsible AI, managers can drive:

- Customer trust and loyalty
- Regulatory compliance
- Long-term business sustainability

Ready to lead with responsible AI? Start implementing ethical AI practices today. Share your thoughts or challenges in the comments!

CORPORATE RESPONSIBILITY IN AI

Chapter-34
Corporate Responsibility in AI

As AI technologies rapidly advance, corporations must embrace their responsibility to ensure ethical development and use of AI systems.

- Corporate responsibility begins with ethical AI development, prioritizing fairness, transparency, and accountability in algorithms.

- Companies must actively work to identify and mitigate biases in their AI systems, ensuring fair treatment for all users.

- Corporate responsibility includes protecting user data and ensuring compliance with data privacy regulations.

- Companies must ensure accountability in AI decision- making processes, providing clarity on how AI systems reach conclusions.

- Engaging stakeholders, including employees, customers, and the community, is vital for ethical AI practices.

- Transparency in AI operations fosters trust. Companies should openly share information about their AI systems and practices.

- Corporate responsibility extends to sustainability, ensuring that AI practices are environmentally friendly and resource-efficient.

- Companies should advocate for policies that promote ethical AI development at local, national, and international levels.

Corporate responsibility in AI is essential for a future where technology benefits everyone. Let's commit to ethical AI practices!

Chapter-35
Combating AI Bias through Governance

AI bias is a pressing issue that organizations must address. Let's explore what AI bias is, why it matters, and how effective governance can help.

- AI bias refers to the unfairness in AI systems, where algorithms produce outcomes that favor one group over another. It can stem from biased data, flawed algorithms, or systemic issues.

- AI bias can lead to discrimination and unfair treatment in critical areas like hiring, lending, law enforcement, and healthcare. This undermines trust and harms affected individuals and communities.

- The consequences of AI bias can include lost opportunities, reinforcement of stereotypes, and legal challenges. It's essential to recognize and address these issues proactively.

- Effective governance practices are crucial for mitigating AI bias. They ensure accountability, transparency, and ethical considerations in AI development and deployment.

- Regular audits of AI algorithms help identify biases. This involves analyzing data, outputs, and decision-making processes to ensure fairness.

- Using diverse and representative datasets during training can minimize bias. Ensure that your training data reflects the real-world diversity of the population.

- Transparency in AI processes allows stakeholders to understand how decisions are made. This builds trust and enables scrutiny to prevent bias.

- Establish clear accountability frameworks. Identify who is responsible for monitoring and addressing bias in AI systems to ensure ethical practices.

AI bias is a critical governance issue that demands attention. What steps are you taking to combat bias in your AI systems?

Share your thoughts and follow us for more insights!

AI ETHICS AND BIAS

Chapter-36

AI Ethics and Bias: Navigating the Challenges

Building Responsible AI for a Fair and Equitable Future

Ethical AI is about ensuring that artificial intelligence systems operate fairly, transparently, and without causing harm. As AI becomes more integrated into our lives, it's essential to address the ethical implications of these technologies.

Key Concerns:

- Bias in AI algorithms
- Data privacy and security
- Transparency and accountability

Bias in AI occurs when algorithms make decisions that are systematically unfair to certain groups. This can happen due to biased training data, flawed models, or a lack of diversity in development teams.

Examples of Bias:

- Facial recognition systems misidentifying people of color.
- Hiring algorithms unfairly favoring certain demographics.

AI ETHICS AND BIAS

AI systems often rely on vast amounts of personal data. Ensuring that this data is handled responsibly and securely is crucial to maintaining user trust and complying with regulations like GDPR.

Key Considerations:

- Consent and transparency in data collection
- Secure storage and processing of sensitive information
- Anonymization and minimization of data use

AI and automation are reshaping industries, leading to concerns about job displacement. While AI can enhance productivity and efficiency, it's important to consider the impact on workers and the need for reskilling.

Key Questions:

- How can we ensure a just transition for displaced workers?
- What role can AI play in creating new job opportunities?

To mitigate ethical risks, companies must prioritize responsible AI development by :

- Implementing fairness audits in AI systems
- Promoting diversity in AI teams
- Ensuring transparency and explainability in AI decisions

The future of AI is not just about innovation—it's about building systems that are ethical, fair, and accountable. By focusing on responsible AI development today, we can create a future where AI benefits everyone.

Chapter-37

Key Principles of AI Governance

Building Trustworthy AI Systems

Introduction to AI Governance

- AI governance refers to the framework of policies, regulations, and practices that guide the ethical and responsible use of AI technologies.
- It ensures that AI systems operate in a manner that is safe, ethical, and beneficial for society.

Transparency

- Transparency means being open about how AI systems work.
- This includes clear communication about data sources, algorithms, and decision-making processes.

Accountability

- Accountability ensures that individuals and organizations are responsible for the outcomes of AI systems.
- It involves having mechanisms to track decisions and hold parties accountable for misuse or harm.

Fairness

- Fairness in AI governance aims to eliminate bias and ensure equitable treatment across different demographics.
- It's crucial to assess and address potential biases in data and algorithms to avoid discrimination.

KEY PRINCIPLES OF AI GOVERNANCE

Inclusivity

- Inclusivity means considering the needs and perspectives of all stakeholders in AI development.
- This includes engaging diverse voices to ensure that AI solutions benefit everyone.

Ethical Use of Data

- Data ethics ensures responsible data collection, usage, and sharing.
- It emphasizes user consent, data privacy, and safeguarding sensitive information.

Continuous Monitoring and Adaptation

- Ongoing monitoring of AI systems is vital to identify and rectify issues as they arise.
- This principle supports the adaptability of governance frameworks in response to technological advances and societal changes.

Implementing these key principles is essential for fostering trust in AI technologies. Together, they help create a foundation for responsible AI governance that benefits society as a whole.

Let's work together to ensure ethical AI development!
Share your thoughts on these principles in the comments below!

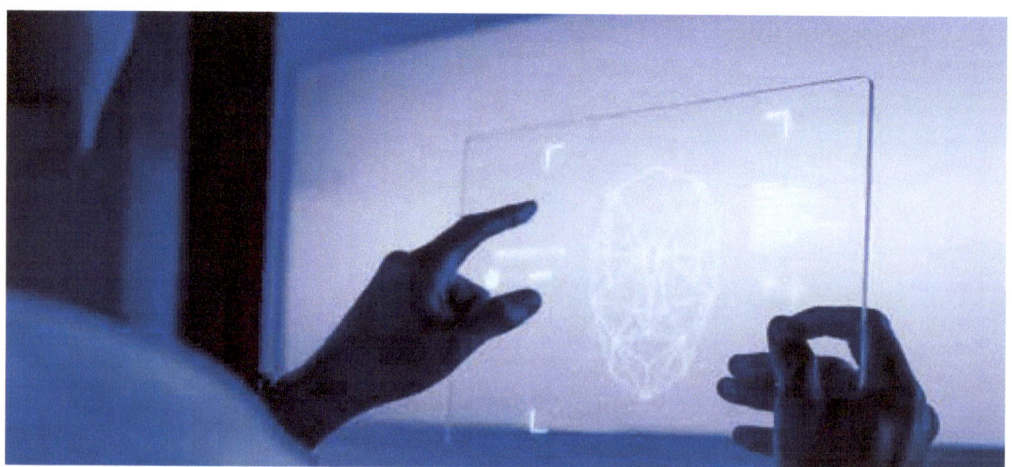

KEY PRINCIPLES OF EFFECTIVE AI GOVERNANCE

Chapter-38

Key Principles of Effective AI Governance

Predicting developments in AI security, including emerging technologies and techniques to mitigate risks.

- AI governance helps organizations manage AI risks and ensures systems operate ethically and transparently. Here are the key principles every company should follow.

- AI should be fair and free from biases. This means treating all users equally and avoiding discrimination.

- Respecting user privacy is essential. AI governance frameworks should protect data and ensure it's used responsibly.

- Users should understand how AI makes decisions. Explainability helps build trust and allows users to challenge incorrect outcomes.

- AI systems must be transparent. Users should understand how AI makes decisions, promoting trust and accountability.

- Organizations need to take responsibility for their AI systems. Clear ownership and accountability help address issues quickly.

- Secure AI systems prevent data breaches and cyber threats. Regular audits and robust security measures are key.

- AI should be designed and deployed ethically, aligning with human rights and societal values. Ethical guidelines prevent misuse.

Building effective AI governance starts with these principles. Ready to lead responsibly?

Follow us for more insights on AI governance.

Chapter-39

Building an AI Governance Framework

Creating a solid governance framework is crucial for responsible AI deployment. Here's a step-by-step guide to get started!

- An effective AI governance framework helps organizations manage risks, ensure compliance, and build trust. Let's break down the essential steps for creating one.

- Form a dedicated team responsible for overseeing AI governance. This team should include diverse stakeholders to bring different perspectives.

- Put in place oversight mechanisms to monitor AI systems. This includes regular reviews, checks for compliance, and a process for reporting issues.

- Ensure that all employees understand the importance of AI governance. Regular training and workshops help promote a culture of responsible AI use.

- Define clear AI governance policies that align with your organization's goals and values. These policies should cover ethical use, data privacy, and compliance.

- Clearly outline the roles and responsibilities within the governance team. This clarity helps ensure accountability and effective oversight.

- Perform regular audits of your AI systems to assess compliance with governance policies and identify areas for improvement.

- Foster an environment where feedback is welcomed. Regularly update your governance framework based on new insights, regulations, and technological advancements.

Building an AI governance framework is a journey, not a destination. Ready to start? Share your thoughts and follow us for more insights!

Chapter-40

AI Governance vs. Regulation: Know the Difference

Understanding the difference between AI governance and regulation is essential for developing responsible AI systems. Let's break it down!

AI governance refers to the internal policies, practices, and frameworks organizations establish to manage their AI systems responsibly. It focuses on ethics, accountability, and transparency.

AI regulation consists of external laws and guidelines set by governments and regulatory bodies. These rules ensure compliance, safety, and fairness in AI deployment across industries.

Scope:

- Governance: Internal focus, tailored to an organization's needs.
- Regulation: External requirements applicable across sectors.

Authority:

- Governance: Driven by organizational leadership.
- Regulation: Enforced by government bodies.

> *AI governance is crucial for fostering trust and ethical behavior within organizations. It allows companies to proactively address risks and ensure alignment with their values.*

AI GOVERNANCE VS. REGULATION: KNOW THE DIFFERENCE

Regulation ensures that AI systems are safe, fair, and accountable. It protects users and society by setting standards and preventing misuse of AI technologies.

- Effective AI governance complements regulation. While governance shapes internal practices, regulation sets the legal framework that guides those practices, promoting responsible AI.

- Organizations may face challenges in balancing governance and regulation, such as compliance costs, keeping up with changing regulations, and fostering a culture of ethics.

Best Practices:

- Foster a culture of transparency and accountability.

- Stay informed about evolving regulations.

- Align internal governance with regulatory standards.

Understanding the difference between AI governance and regulation is key to fostering responsible AI use. How is your organization addressing both?

Join the discussion and share your insights!

HOW AI GOVERNANCE BUILDS TRUST WITH USERS

Chapter-41

Building Trust Through AI Governance

Trust is essential for the successful adoption of AI technologies. Let's explore how effective AI governance fosters trust with users.

- Trust in AI systems is crucial for user adoption. When users feel secure and confident in how AI operates, they are more likely to engage with it.

- Transparency means clearly communicating how AI systems work, including data sources and decision-making processes. It helps users understand and trust the technology.

- Establishing clear policies around data usage, privacy, and user rights is vital. When users know their information is handled responsibly, trust is strengthened.

- Ethical AI practices, like avoiding bias and ensuring fairness, are essential for building trust. Users expect AI systems to operate responsibly and ethically.

- Involving stakeholders in the governance process fosters collaboration and transparency. This ensures diverse perspectives are considered, enhancing trust.

- Educating users about AI technology, its benefits, and its limitations promotes informed usage and trust. Knowledge empowers users to engage confidently.

- Conducting regular audits of AI systems and soliciting user feedback shows commitment to accountability and improvement, reinforcing trust over time.

- Creating a culture of trust within organizations promotes responsible AI practices. When employees value trust, it reflects in how they develop and implement AI.

Building trust through AI governance is essential for user engagement. What steps are you taking to enhance trust in your AI systems?

Chapter-42

AI Governance: Why It Matters

AI is transforming our world, but without proper governance, it can bring risks. Let's explore why AI governance is crucial!

- Without governance, AI can be biased, leading to unfair outcomes. AI governance ensures fairness and equal treatment for everyone.

- AI governance builds trust. When users know their data is safe and the AI is fair, they're more likely to engage and adopt AI solutions.

- Governance doesn't just prevent risks—it encourages responsible innovation. It helps companies build better, safer AI products.

- AI processes massive amounts of data, raising privacy concerns. Governance frameworks set rules to protect personal information.

- Governance helps companies comply with laws and avoid legal problems. This is crucial as AI regulations are growing worldwide.

- As AI continues to grow, having robust governance frameworks will ensure it benefits everyone while minimizing risks.

> *How to Start with AI Governance:*
>
> 1. Define clear policies
> 2. Monitor and audit AI systems
> 3. Promote transparency

Want to learn more about responsible AI practices? Follow us for more insights!
Share your thoughts: Why do you think AI governance is essential?

THE ROLE OF GOVERNMENTS IN AI GOVERNANCE

Chapter-43
Corporate The Role of Governments in AI Governance

As artificial intelligence rapidly evolves, governments play a critical role in establishing frameworks for its governance. Let's explore how they influence AI's future.

- Governments establish legal frameworks to ensure AI systems operate within the law, protecting citizens' rights and freedoms.

- Regulations help define standards for AI development and deployment, ensuring safety, reliability, and fairness in AI systems.

- Governments advocate for ethical AI practices, promoting transparency, accountability, and inclusivity in AI development.

- Government funding for AI research drives innovation and ensures ethical considerations are prioritized in technological advancements.

- Governments collaborate on international standards for AI, addressing global challenges and fostering responsible AI use worldwide.

- Regulatory bodies must ensure AI systems are safe for public use, mitigating risks associated with emerging technologies.

- Governments are tasked with addressing ethical concerns like bias, discrimination, and privacy in AI systems, ensuring fairness for all.

- Public engagement is crucial. Governments must involve citizens in discussions about AI governance to reflect societal values and priorities.

The role of governments in AI governance is essential for a future where AI benefits society while upholding ethical standards. Let's work together for responsible AI!

Chapter-44
The Role of Stakeholders in AI Governance
Understanding Responsibilities in the AI Ecosystem

AI governance involves multiple stakeholders, each with distinct roles and responsibilities. Collaboration among these parties is essential for effective and responsible AI deployment.

Developers:
Developers are responsible for designing and building AI systems.

- Implementing ethical guidelines during development.
- Ensuring data quality and security.
- Conducting bias assessments and testing.

Data Scientists:
Data scientists play a crucial role in analyzing and interpreting data used in AI.

- Selecting relevant data for training AI models.
- Identifying and mitigating biases in datasets.
- Ensuring transparency in data usage.

Regulatory Bodies:
Regulatory bodies set the framework for AI governance and compliance.

- Establishing laws and guidelines for AI deployment.
- Monitoring compliance with ethical standards.
- Enforcing penalties for non-compliance.

THE ROLE OF STAKEHOLDERS

Businesses and Organizations:
Businesses must implement AI governance within their operations.

- Developing internal AI ethics policies.
- Training employees on responsible AI use.
- Engaging with stakeholders to ensure compliance.

Users:
Users interact with AI systems and provide valuable feedback.

- Understanding how AI affects decision-making.
- Reporting issues or biases encountered.
- Advocating for transparency and fairness.

Researchers and Academics:
Researchers contribute to the advancement of AI ethics and governance.

- Conducting studies on AI impacts and effectiveness.
- Publishing findings to inform best practices.
- Collaborating with stakeholders to improve AI systems.

Civil Society and Advocacy Groups:
Civil society and advocacy groups ensure public interests are represented.

- Advocating for ethical AI practices.
- Raising awareness of potential risks and harms.
- Engaging in public discourse around AI governance.

Effective AI governance requires collaboration among all stakeholders. By understanding their roles and responsibilities, we can foster a safer and more ethical AI ecosystem.

What role do you play in AI governance?
Share your thoughts or experiences in the comments!

Chapter-45

The Future of AI Governance: Emerging Trends to Watch

Explore the latest trends shaping the future of AI governance and how they will impact organizations worldwide.

- International standards for AI governance are gaining momentum. These guidelines aim to ensure consistent ethical practices across borders, fostering trust and collaboration.

- Companies are increasingly adopting ethical AI audits to assess their systems' fairness, transparency, and accountability. This proactive approach helps identify and mitigate risks.

- Cross-border collaborations in AI governance are emerging as countries recognize the need for shared frameworks. This cooperation enhances global efforts to regulate AI effectively.

- Organizations are establishing AI ethics boards to guide responsible AI practices. These boards ensure diverse perspectives and accountability in decision-making processes.

- AI governance is evolving rapidly. Organizations are embracing a culture of continuous learning to adapt their governance frameworks to keep pace with technological advancements and societal expectations.

- The future of AI governance will be shaped by international standards, ethical audits, collaborative efforts, and diverse perspectives. Staying informed and adaptable is key for organizations..

- The growth of Regulatory Technology (RegTech) tools is helping organizations automate compliance and monitoring of AI regulations, making governance more efficient and effective.

- Stakeholder engagement in AI governance is becoming more crucial. Companies are involving customers, employees, and communities in discussions about ethical AI practices.

What trends do you see shaping the future of AI governance? Share your thoughts and insights in the comments below!

Let's continue the conversation on responsible AI!

Chapter-46

Overcoming Challenges in AI Governance

Navigating the complexities of AI governance can be challenging. Here are common issues and tips on how to overcome them.

- AI governance faces various challenges, including regulatory compliance, data privacy, bias, and more. Let's explore these challenges and effective strategies to tackle them.
- Staying compliant with ever-evolving regulations can be difficult. Organizations must keep up with local and international laws regarding AI usage.
- Establish a dedicated compliance team that regularly reviews and updates policies. Engage legal experts to stay informed about regulatory changes.
- Protecting user data is paramount. AI systems often require large datasets, raising concerns about how this data is handled and secured.
- Implement strong data governance policies, use encryption, and ensure transparency about data usage to build user trust.
- Bias in AI can lead to unfair treatment of individuals or groups. Identifying and mitigating bias is essential for ethical AI use.
- Conduct regular audits of AI algorithms and use diverse training datasets to identify and correct bias in AI models.
- Establishing accountability in AI decision-making can be challenging. It's crucial to identify who is responsible for AI outcomes.
- Clearly define roles and responsibilities within your AI governance framework. Use accountability logs to track decisions made by AI systems.
- Navigating ethical standards across different countries can be complex. Variations in cultural values and regulations pose challenges.
- Collaborate with international organizations and stakeholders to develop shared ethical guidelines and practices for AI deployment.

Overcoming challenges in AI governance requires proactive strategies and collaboration. How do you approach these challenges in your organization?
Join the discussion and follow us for more insights!

Chapter-47
The Future of AI/ML: Trends and Predictions

Explore Emerging Trends Shaping the Future of AI/ML

Explainable AI (XAI): Making AI Transparent
One of the biggest challenges in AI today is its "black-box" nature, where even developers don't fully understand how AI models make decisions. Explainable AI (XAI) seeks to make AI systems more transparent and understandable, fostering trust in AI by explaining how decisions are made.

Why It Matters:

- Builds trust in AI systems
- Promotes ethical AI use
- Enables better decision-making with AI insights

Federated Learning: Decentralized AI Training
Federated learning allows AI models to be trained across multiple devices without the need to share sensitive data. This trend is gaining traction, particularly in industries like healthcare and finance, where data privacy is critical. The models learn collaboratively without compromising user privacy.

Why It Matters:

- Enhances data privacy
- Reduces risks associated with data breaches
- Enables collaborative learning across decentralized systems

AI in Edge Computing: Smarter Devices
AI is moving closer to where data is generated—on edge devices like smartphones, IoT devices, and drones. Edge AI reduces latency, increases efficiency, and enables real-time decision-making without relying on cloud connectivity. Industries like autonomous vehicles and smart cities are embracing this trend.

Why It Matters:

- Enables real-time processing and decision-making
- Powers intelligent IoT and autonomous systems

AI for Sustainability: Tackling Climate Change
AI is playing a crucial role in addressing climate change and environmental sustainability. From optimizing energy consumption to predicting natural disasters, AI models are being leveraged to solve complex environmental challenges, making industries greener and more sustainable.

Why It Matters:

- Reduces carbon footprints
- Optimizes resource usage
- Helps predict and mitigate climate disasters

AI/ML TRENDS AND PREDICTIONS

AI Democratization: Making AI Accessible

AI democratization refers to making AI technology accessible to everyone, not just tech giants. Tools like low-code/no-code platforms are enabling non-experts to build AI solutions, allowing small businesses and startups to leverage AI for innovation. This trend is creating new opportunities across industries.

Why It Matters:

- Broadens access to AI tools
- Spurs innovation across industries
- Empowers non-technical users to create AI solutions

Future Prediction: AI Co-Evolution with Humans

As AI continues to evolve, it will not replace humans but augment human capabilities. The future will see more collaboration between humans and AI, where AI handles repetitive tasks and humans focus on creativity, innovation, and emotional intelligence. AI will be our co-pilot in solving global challenges.

Why It Matters:

- AI complements human abilities
- Helps solve complex problems that require both AI and human intelligence
- Unlocks new opportunities for creativity and innovation

The future of AI/ML is bright, with emerging trends reshaping industries and society. As we move forward, staying informed about these trends and ethical considerations will be crucial. What are your thoughts on the future of AI/ML?

ETHICAL AI DESIGN PRINCIPLES

Chapter-48
Ethical AI Design Principles
Guiding Frameworks for Responsible AI Development

Ethical AI design is essential for creating systems that are fair, transparent, and beneficial. Key design principles guide developers in making responsible choices throughout the AI lifecycle.

User-Centered Design:
Prioritize the needs and values of users throughout the design process.

- Understanding user contexts and behaviors.
- Engaging users in the development process.
- Designing for accessibility and inclusivity.

Transparency:
Ensure clarity about how AI systems work and make decisions.

- Provide clear documentation of AI functionalities.
- Explain algorithms and data usage to users.
- Enable users to understand AI-driven outcomes.

Avoiding Bias:
Design AI systems to minimize bias and ensure fairness.

- Use diverse datasets for training.
- Regularly audit algorithms for bias.
- Involve diverse teams in the development process.

The AI Compass: Security, Ethics, and Leadership

ETHICAL AI DESIGN PRINCIPLES

Accountability:

Establish clear accountability for AI system outcomes.

- Define roles and responsibilities in development.
- Implement mechanisms for monitoring and evaluation.
- Create pathways for addressing harm caused by AI.

Privacy and Data Protection:

Incorporate strong privacy measures in AI design.

- Collect only necessary data.
- Use encryption and secure data storage.
- Provide users with control over their data.

Continuous Improvement:

Implement mechanisms for ongoing evaluation and improvement of AI systems.

- Gather user feedback post-launch.
- Adapt systems based on real-world performance.
- Stay updated with ethical AI standards and regulations.

Collaboration and Multi-Stakeholder Engagement:

Engage with various stakeholders in the design process.

- Collaborate with ethicists, users, and domain experts.
- Create forums for public discussion on AI ethics.
- Involve community voices in decision-making.

Adhering to ethical AI design principles is crucial for building trust and ensuring the responsible use of technology. By prioritizing user needs and ethical considerations, we can create AI systems that benefit

What ethical design principles guide your AI projects?

Share your insights or experiences in the comments!

Chapter-49

International Cooperation for AI Ethics

As AI technology transcends borders, international cooperation is essential for developing ethical standards that guide its use globally.

- AI poses unique challenges that require a unified response. Global standards ensure fairness, transparency, and accountability in AI systems worldwide.

- Organizations like the UN, OECD, and IEEE play vital roles in fostering international dialogue and developing ethical AI policies.

- By sharing knowledge and best practices, countries can learn from each other's successes and failures in AI governance and ethics.

- Countries should develop joint policies and guidelines that address specific ethical concerns related to AI while respecting cultural differences.

- Countries must work together to establish collaborative frameworks that allow for shared best practices and ethical guidelines in AI.

- AI technologies raise ethical issues that impact everyone, from privacy and bias to surveillance. Global cooperation is essential to tackle these challenges.

- International cooperation encourages transparency in AI development, allowing for shared accountability across nations.

- Cross-border dialogues among governments, industries, and civil societies are crucial for harmonizing AI ethics across jurisdictions.

The ethical use of AI is a global challenge that requires collective action. Let's work together to build an ethical future for AI.

Chapter-50
Global Regulatory Landscape for AI Governance

Emerging Regulations and Standards Around the World.

As AI technologies evolve, so does the need for effective governance. Regulations are emerging globally to address ethical, security, and accountability concerns in AI applications.

The European Union (EU) Approach:
The EU is at the forefront of AI regulation with its proposed AI Act.

- Risk-based classification of AI systems.
- Stricter regulations for high-risk applications.
- Emphasis on transparency, accountability, and human oversight.

United States Regulatory Landscape:
In the US, AI regulation is evolving through a patchwork of state and federal initiatives.

- Federal guidance from agencies like the FTC.
- State-level privacy laws like the California Consumer Privacy Act (CCPA).
- Focus on innovation while ensuring accountability.

United Kingdom's Regulatory Approach:
The UK is developing its AI governance framework through a combination of principles and guidelines.

- Emphasis on innovation-friendly regulations.
- Focus on the Data Protection Act and its implications for AI.
- Consultation with stakeholders to ensure practical applicability.

GLOBAL REGULATORY LANDSCAPE

Asia-Pacific Regulations:
Asia-Pacific countries are taking diverse approaches to AI governance.
- Singapore: Proactive regulatory sandbox for AI innovation.
- China: Comprehensive regulations emphasizing state control and security.
- Japan: Guidelines focusing on ethical AI development and human-centric values.

Global Collaborations:
International collaboration is crucial for effective AI governance.
- OECD AI Principles: Promoting responsible AI.
- Global Partnership on AI (GPAI): Fostering international cooperation.
- IEEE Standards: Developing technical standards for ethical AI.

Key Challenges in Global Regulation:
Despite progress, several challenges remain in AI regulation:
- Harmonizing regulations across regions.
- Balancing innovation with safety and ethical considerations.
- Addressing rapid technological advancements that outpace regulation.

Future Directions in AI Regulation:
The future of AI regulation may involve:
- Greater standardization across regions.
- Continuous updates to regulations in response to evolving technologies.
- Inclusion of diverse stakeholder perspectives to shape effective governance.

As the global regulatory landscape for AI continues to evolve, collaboration and innovation are key. Staying informed about emerging regulations will be essential for responsible AI development.

What are your thoughts on the global regulatory landscape for AI?
Share your insights and experiences in the comments!

AI Ethics, Future Trends, and Final Thoughts

Chapter-51
Ensuring Responsible AI: Ethics, Bias, and Fairness
Explore best practices for AI ethics and responsible adoption

1. The Impact of Unethical AI
- Bias and discrimination
- Lack of transparency
- Privacy violations
- Unintended consequences

2. Foundational Principles
- Respect for autonomy
- Beneficence (do good)
- Non-maleficence (do no harm)
- Justice and fairness

3. Addressing Bias in AI
- Data quality and diversity
- Human oversight
- Algorithmic auditing
- Continuous monitoring

4. Promoting AI Fairness
- Data-driven decision-making
- Regular auditing
- Transparency and explainability
- Feedback mechanisms

5. Demystifying AI Decision-Making
- Model interpretability
- Model-agnostic explanations
- Feature attribution
- Transparent communication

6. Human-Centric AI Governance
- Human-in-the-loop
- Incident response plans
- Regular auditing
- Accountability mechanisms

7. Establishing AI Ethics Standards
- EU AI Ethics Guidelines
- AI Now Institute's Ethics Guidelines
- IEEE Global Initiative on Ethics of Autonomous and Intelligent Systems

8. Putting AI Ethics into Practice
- Conduct AI ethics assessments
- Develop AI ethics policies
- Establish AI governance structures
- Provide AI ethics training

Chapter-52

How Companies Are Leading in AI Governance

Explore how companies are setting the standard for AI governance through effective frameworks and practices.

Effective AI governance is crucial for building trust, ensuring ethical use, and meeting regulatory requirements. Leading companies prioritize these aspects for success.

Microsoft

Microsoft has established an AI ethics committee that guides their AI strategy, focusing on transparency, accountability, and user privacy. Their "AI Principles" ensure ethical practices.

Google

Google promotes responsible AI development through their AI Principles. They prioritize fairness, transparency, and user privacy, ensuring their systems are designed to be beneficial for all.

IBM

IBM emphasizes ethical AI through their AI Fairness 360 toolkit, which helps developers detect and mitigate bias in AI models. They also provide transparency reports to stakeholders.

COMPANIES SETTING THE BAR FOR AI GOVERNANCE

Salesforce

Salesforce has implemented an AI ethics board that focuses on ethical considerations in AI product development. They aim to build trust with customers through responsible AI usage.

OpenAI

OpenAI prioritizes safety and ethical use in AI development. Their governance model includes rigorous safety protocols and public input, ensuring responsible deployment of AI technologies.

Meta

Meta has created an independent oversight board to review and provide guidance on AI-related content decisions. This enhances transparency and accountability in their governance approach.

Leading companies demonstrate that robust AI governance frameworks result in better decision-making, enhanced trust, and compliance with regulations. Emulating their practices can benefit all organizations.

What steps is your organization taking to enhance AI governance? Let's discuss best practices and share insights to foster responsible AI!

Engage with us for more information on AI governance.

Chapter-53

Safe Cognitive and Sovereign AI Symposium

Explore the latest innovations, discussions, and challenges around ensuring safe and sovereign AI. Welcome to the Safe Cognitive and Sovereign AI Symposium!

- Safe Cognitive AI refers to systems that think, learn, and make decisions like humans, with safeguards to prevent harmful actions.

- Sovereign AI emphasizes control, independence, and ownership of AI systems within a nation, free from external influence.

- As AI grows more powerful, safety becomes paramount. AI systems must be designed with ethical safeguards to prevent misuse or unintended consequences.

- Governments play a crucial role in defining policies that protect their digital sovereignty and ensure responsible AI development.

- Cognitive AI must align with human values to ensure fairness, transparency, and respect for individual rights.

- International collaboration between governments, industries, and researchers is essential to developing safe AI systems for the future.

- Sovereign AI has major implications for national security. Controlling AI systems within a country's borders can protect critical infrastructure and data.

The future of AI depends on our collective efforts to ensure its safe, ethical, and sovereign development. Let's continue to push for innovation with responsibility.

Chapter-54

Future Trends in AI Governance
Exploring Emerging Trends in Governance, Ethics, and Security

AI governance is evolving rapidly in response to technological advancements. Let's explore the key future trends shaping the landscape of AI governance, ethics, and security.

Decentralized Governance Models:
Decentralized governance models are gaining traction.

- Distributed decision-making reduces central authority.
- Encourages innovation through community-driven approaches.
- Greater stakeholder participation enhances accountability.

Impact of Quantum Computing on Security:
Quantum computing poses both challenges and opportunities for AI security.

- Potential to break traditional encryption methods.
- Necessitates the development of quantum-resistant algorithms.
- Enables faster processing of complex AI models.

Increased Focus on AI Transparency:
Transparency in AI decision-making processes is becoming paramount.

- Explainable AI (XAI) to understand AI decisions.
- Public reporting on AI system performance and impacts.
- Open data initiatives to promote accountability.

FUTURE TRENDS IN AI GOVERNANCE

Rise of Ethical AI Frameworks:
Ethical AI frameworks are emerging as essential for responsible AI development.

- Fairness and transparency in AI algorithms.
- Bias mitigation and inclusive design principles.
- Accountability mechanisms for AI outcomes.

AI Governance in Global Collaboration:
International collaboration is critical for effective AI governance.

- Shared regulatory frameworks across countries.
- Joint initiatives to tackle global challenges like climate change.
- Cross-border partnerships for AI research and ethics.

AI Regulation and Compliance:
Anticipate stricter regulations and compliance requirements for AI systems.

- Development of comprehensive AI regulations.
- Increased emphasis on data privacy and protection laws.
- Standardization of AI governance practices.

Addressing the Skills Gap in AI Governance:
The demand for skilled professionals in AI governance is growing.

- Training programs for AI ethics and governance.
- Cross-disciplinary approaches combining tech, law, and ethics.
- Promoting diversity in AI leadership roles.

The future of AI governance is shaped by emerging trends that promote ethical, secure, and inclusive AI systems. By embracing these trends, we can create a responsible AI ecosystem for all.

What trends in AI governance do you find most compelling?
Share your thoughts and predictions in the comments!

Chapter-55

AI Talent War Heats Up!

The competition for top AI talent is intensifying as companies vie to lead the AI revolution. Here's why AI talent is becoming the hottest commodity and how you can stay ahead.

Surge in Demand

AI skills are in high demand across industries. From startups to tech giants, everyone needs AI experts to drive innovation and maintain a competitive edge.

In-Demand AI Skills

- Machine Learning & Deep Learning
- Natural Language Processing (NLP)
- Data Science & Analytics
- AI Ethics & Governance

Talent Shortage Challenge

Discover how combining voice technology with GPT models can creates despite the growing demand, there is a shortage of qualified AI professionals. Companies are facing challenges in finding and retaining top talented!

Attracting Top Talent

- Offer Competitive Salaries and Benefits
- Foster a Culture of Innovation
- Invest in Training and Development
- Provide Opportunities for Career Growth

Building Your AI Dream Team

Focus on creating an inclusive and collaborative environment. Encourage continuous learning and provide clear career progression paths to retain top talent.

How Are You Addressing the AI Talent War?

Share your strategies for attracting and retaining AI talent. Comment below or DM me to discuss how we can navigate this talent challenge together!

Chapter-56

The Future of AI/ML: Trends and Predictions

Explore Emerging Trends Shaping the Future of AI/ML

Explainable AI (XAI): Making AI Transparent

One of the biggest challenges in AI today is its "black-box" nature, where even developers don't fully understand how AI models make decisions. Explainable AI (XAI) seeks to make AI systems more transparent and understandable, fostering trust in AI by explaining how decisions are made.

Why It Matters:

- Builds trust in AI systems
- Promotes ethical AI use
- Enables better decision-making with AI insights

Federated Learning: Decentralized AI Training

Federated learning allows AI models to be trained across multiple devices without the need to share sensitive data. This trend is gaining traction, particularly in industries like healthcare and finance, where data privacy is critical. The models learn collaboratively without compromising user privacy.

Why It Matters:

- Enhances data privacy
- Reduces risks associated with data breaches
- Enables collaborative learning across decentralized systems

AI in Edge Computing: Smarter Devices

AI is moving closer to where data is generated—on edge devices like smartphones, IoT devices, and drones. Edge AI reduces latency, increases efficiency, and enables real-time decision-making without relying on cloud connectivity. Industries like autonomous vehicles and smart cities are embracing this trend.

Why It Matters:

- Enables real-time processing and decision-making
- Powers intelligent IoT and autonomous systems

AI for Sustainability: Tackling Climate Change

AI is playing a crucial role in addressing climate change and environmental sustainability. From optimizing energy consumption to predicting natural disasters, AI models are being leveraged to solve complex environmental challenges, making industries greener and more sustainable.

Why It Matters:

- Reduces carbon footprints
- Optimizes resource usage
- Helps predict and mitigate climate disasters

AI/ML TRENDS AND PREDICTIONS

AI Democratization: Making AI Accessible
AI democratization refers to making AI technology accessible to everyone, not just tech giants. Tools like low-code/no-code platforms are enabling non-experts to build AI solutions, allowing small businesses and startups to leverage AI for innovation. This trend is creating new opportunities across industries.

Why It Matters:

- Broadens access to AI tools
- Spurs innovation across industries
- Empowers non-technical users to create AI solutions

Future Prediction: AI Co-Evolution with Humans
As AI continues to evolve, it will not replace humans but augment human capabilities. The future will see more collaboration between humans and AI, where AI handles repetitive tasks and humans focus on creativity, innovation, and emotional intelligence. AI will be our co-pilot in solving global challenges.

Why It Matters:

- AI complements human abilities
- Helps solve complex problems that require both AI and human intelligence
- Unlocks new opportunities for creativity and innovation

The future of AI/ML is bright, with emerging trends reshaping industries and society. As we move forward, staying informed about these trends and ethical considerations will be crucial. What are your thoughts on the future of AI/ML?

AI-POWERED SKILLS TO ACQUIRE FOR CAREER ADVANCEMENT

Chapter-57

Future-Proof Your Career with AI-Powered Skills

Stay ahead in the industry with in-demand AI skills.

1. Master ML Fundamentals
- Data preprocessing
- Algorithm selection
- Model training
- Deployment

2. Unlock NLP Potential
- Text analysis
- Language modeling
- Sentiment analysis
- Chatbots

3. Tell Stories with Data
- Data wrangling
- Statistical analysis
- Visualization tools
- Insight generation

4. Ensure Responsible AI
- Bias detection
- Transparency
- Fairness analysis
- Regulatory compliance

5. Dive into DL and Neural Networks
- Convolutional neural networks (CNNs)
- Generative adversarial networks (GANs)
- Recurrent neural networks (RNNs)
- Transfer learning

6. Transforming Industries
- Healthcare: predictive analytics
- Marketing: personalized recommendations
- Finance: risk analysis

7. Unlock New Career Opportunities
- AI engineer
- Business analyst
- Data scientist
- AI researcher

8. Develop Your AI Skills
- Online courses (Coursera, edX)
- Books and research papers
- Certifications (Google, Microsoft)
- Professional networks

The AI Compass: Security, Ethics, and Leadership

Chapter-58
AI/ML for Social Good
How AI/ML is Addressing Global Challenges and Creating a Positive Impact.

AI is transforming healthcare by improving diagnostics, treatment, and patient outcomes. For example, AI-driven tools can detect diseases like cancer in their early stages, enabling timely intervention and saving lives. AI-powered robotic surgeries are also making operations safer and more precise.

Impact:
- Early disease detection
- Precision medicine
- Improved patient outcomes

AI is breaking down barriers to education by creating personalized learning experiences for students. Tools like adaptive learning platforms adjust to students' needs, helping them learn at their own pace. AI is also enabling access to quality education for underserved communities worldwide.

Impact:
- Personalized learning paths
- Access to quality education
- Bridging the education gap

AI is helping to combat climate change by optimizing energy use, predicting natural disasters, and promoting sustainable practices. From reducing emissions to preserving biodiversity, AI is providing critical insights to help protect our planet.

Impact:
- Optimized energy consumption
- Predictive models for climate events
- Promoting sustainable practices

AI is enhancing social services by identifying areas of need, optimizing resource allocation, and improving access to essential services like housing and welfare. From food distribution to disaster relief, AI is empowering communities and making a tangible impact on people's lives.

Impact:
- Better resource distribution
- Optimized public service delivery
- Supporting vulnerable populations

AI/ML FOR SOCIAL GOOD

AI is being used to monitor and protect wildlife, track deforestation, and promote biodiversity. From using drones to track endangered species to satellite imagery analyzing environmental changes, AI is a powerful tool in conservation efforts.

Impact:

- Wildlife protection
- Forest conservation
- Promoting biodiversity

AI is helping humanitarian organizations respond faster and more effectively to crises. From mapping disaster zones using satellite imagery to predicting the spread of diseases in refugee camps, AI is saving lives by speeding up response efforts.

Impact:

- Faster disaster response
- Efficient resource allocation
- Saving lives in crisis situations

AI/ML has the power to address some of the world's most pressing challenges, from healthcare and education to climate action and crisis response. As we move forward, ensuring responsible AI development will be key to maximizing its positive impact.

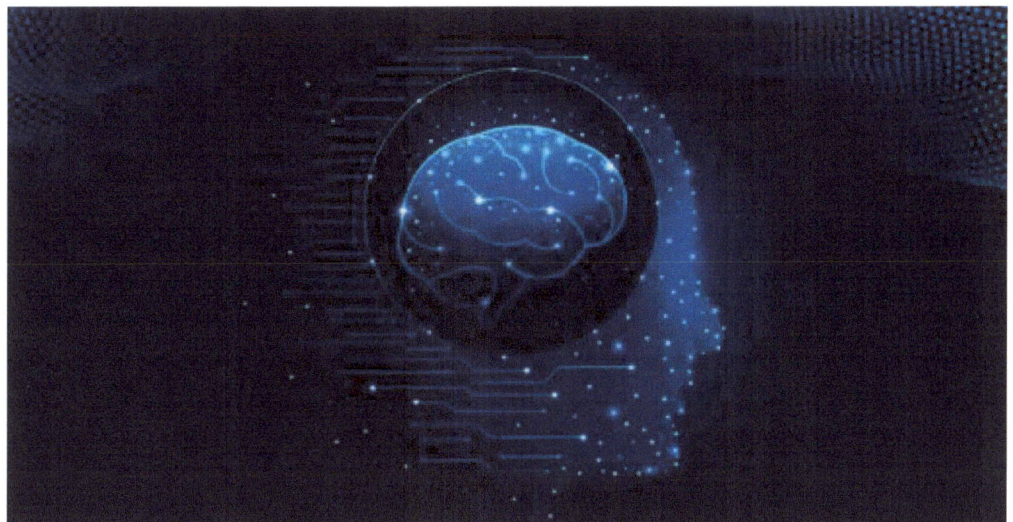

Real-World Examples and Case Studies

Chapter-59

Real-World Case Studies in AI Governance

Lessons from Successful Frameworks Around the Globe

We will explore key lessons learned from various organizations and countries

Canada's AI Framework

Canada's Directive on Automated Decision-Making ensures transparency and accountability. Key elements include risk assessments and clear communication about AI decisions.

Lessons Learned:

- Clear guidelines foster trust.
- Regular audits can mitigate risks.
- Engage stakeholders early in the process.

European Union AI Act

The EU's AI Act aims to create a comprehensive regulatory framework for AI. It categorizes AI applications based on risk and imposes strict obligations on high-risk AI systems.

Lessons Learned:

- Proactive regulation is key to innovation.
- Risk-based approach promotes responsible use.
- Collaboration among member states enhances effectiveness.

REAL-WORLD CASE STUDIES

Microsoft's AI Principles

Microsoft's AI governance framework focuses on fairness, reliability, privacy, and inclusivity. They emphasize ethical AI development and provide resources for responsible AI usage.

Lessons Learned:

- Clear ethical guidelines enhance corporate responsibility.
- Transparency builds customer trust.
- Employee training on AI ethics is essential.

Singapore's Smart Nation Initiative

Singapore promotes AI governance through its Smart Nation initiative, focusing on responsible AI deployment. They incorporate public feedback in AI system designs to ensure societal acceptance.

Lessons Learned:

- Public engagement leads to better outcomes.
- Collaboration between public and private sectors enhances innovation.
- Regular updates based on feedback are crucial.

These case studies highlight the importance of effective AI governance.

By learning from successful frameworks, organizations can foster trust and responsible AI use.

What are your thoughts on these case studies?

Share your experiences or insights on AI governance in the comments!

The AI Compass: Security, Ethics, and Leadership

Shaping the Future with Responsible AI Leadership.

As we close this journey through The AI Compass: Security, Ethics, and Leadership, one message should resonate with you above all: the future of artificial intelligence holds immense promise but demands equally profound responsibility. Throughout this book, we've navigated the essential elements of AI, from its foundational principles and industry-transforming applications to the critical practices of securing and governing these powerful technologies. However, the journey does not end here; it evolves with each decision we make.

In my experience as an AI leader and entrepreneur, I have seen firsthand the dual-edged nature of technology. AI has the power to revolutionize industries, improve lives, and create unprecedented economic growth, but only when wielded with foresight, ethical awareness, and a commitment to the greater good. This requires not only technical expertise but also a deep sense of responsibility and empathy for the people impacted by these advancements. My work at Kazma Technology and as the founder of ChatWeft has been guided by these principles, always emphasizing the importance of AI ethics, compliance, security, and governance.

At its core, responsible AI is about more than mitigating risks; it's about setting a new standard for trust and integrity in technology. It's about fostering a mindset where ethical considerations are the starting point of every project, where diverse teams build systems free of biases, and where transparency becomes a bridge to public trust. I encourage you to carry these values forward, to be advocates for a safer, more ethical future in which AI empowers rather than exploits.

As leaders, innovators, and enthusiasts, you have a choice: to passively watch AI shape our world or to actively guide its evolution with wisdom and compassion. Lead with courage. Innovate with conscience. Protect what matters—not just in terms of data and intellectual property but in terms of human dignity and collective well-being.

Remember, progress doesn't mean compromising on values. AI's true potential is realized when its capabilities are aligned with human-centric values—enhancing lives, protecting the vulnerable, fostering social good, and creating opportunities for all. The real testament to our time will not be the technologies we create but how we use them to build a world that respects, empowers, and uplifts every individual.

So, stay informed, stay vigilant, and most importantly, stay committed to ethical leadership. Each step you take contributes to a future where AI is not feared as an instrument of unchecked power, but embraced as a beacon of innovation that serves humanity.

The journey is ongoing, and you are part of a global movement that champions a better, smarter, and more secure world. Together, let's create an era where AI not only transforms industries but enriches human experience—an era that our future generations will look back on with gratitude and pride.

Thank you for embarking on this journey with me. Your leadership, driven by ethics and vision, will make all the difference. The future of AI is ours to shape—let's do it wisely and with unwavering resolve.

www.ingramcontent.com/pod-product-compliance
Lightning Source LLC
Chambersburg PA
CBHW040317220526
45473CB00009B/2474